City Living

City Living

CREATIVE DESIGN IDEAS FOR THE NEW URBAN HOME

Sharne Algotsson

ROCKPORT PUBLISHERS

First published in the United States of America by
Rockport Publishers, Inc.
33 Commercial Street
Gloucester, Massachusetts 01930-5089
Telephone: (978) 282-9590
Fax: (978) 283-2742
www.rockpub.com

Library of Congress Cataloging-in-Publication Data
Algotsson, Sharne.
   City living: creative design ideas for the new urban home / Sharne
Algotsson.
      p.   cm.
   ISBN 1-56496-478-7 (hardcover)
   1. Interior decoration. 2. Room layout (Dwellings) 3. City and town
life. I. Title.
   NK2113.A54 2003
   747.29173'2—dc21   2003002181

ISBN 1-56496-478-7
10 9 8 7 6 5 4 3 2 1

Design: Stoltze Design
Cover Image: Luke White/The Interior Archive
Copyeditor: Pamela Elizian
Proofreader: Stacey Ann Follin

Special thanks to *Homes of Color* magazine for the images on the following pages: 2, 64, 69, 84, 103 and 124.

ACKNOWLEDGMENTS

Many thanks to the editors at Rockport Publishers—Mary Ann Hall for her guidance and patience through the difficult phases of bringing my love of the city to the written page, and Paula Munier for sharing my enthusiasm for the subject of urban living from the very beginning. I would like to thank photo editor Betsy Gammons whose keen eye for the right photography helped make this book more beautiful than I had envisioned. A special thank you to my daughter, Vanessa Algotsson, whose chosen path as a writer is a wonderful stroke of luck, as she is always the first to proof anything I write.

To all the photographers whose beautiful images are a story in themselves and together tell the global story of city living, thanks so much. Special thanks to Corrice Gwynn and *Homes of Color* magazine for the images by Nester Hernandez, Penny Shaw Kubatana Gallery, and International Vision Gallery.

Finally, an extra-special thank-you to my husband, Jan, who is always there to support me through all of my endeavors from beginning to end.

CONTENTS

INTRODUCTION **What Is City Style?** / 8

CHAPTER 1 **Architecture, The First Impression of the City** / 14

CHAPTER 2 **The Illusion of Space** / 36

CHAPTER 3 **City Comforts** / 54

CHAPTER 4 **An Urban Home in Every Sense** / 72

CHAPTER 5 **Places to Gather** / 90

CHAPTER 6 **Living and Working at Home** / 104

CHAPTER 7 **Places Just to Be** / 120

RESOURCES / 140

PHOTOGRAPHER CREDITS / 143

ABOUT THE AUTHOR / 144

From Asia to Europe, urbanites
find comfort in the convenience
of walkable cities with easy
access to the marketplace, work,
and play.

WHAT IS CITY STYLE?

When I was 13, growing up in Philadelphia, I persuaded my mother
to let me take guitar lessons. Every Saturday of that spring, summer, and fall, my mother and I would walk to the studio. In that
neighborhood of artists, a magical cacophony of classical piano,
operatic voice exercises, and saxophone melodies could always be
heard floating through the windows of magnificent 19th-century
town houses onto the sidewalks. Although my knowledge of the
guitar has long since disappeared, the recollection of those
Saturday morning walks, serenaded by musical breezes amid the
powerful yet graceful architecture, forever fills me with a warm
memory of my first feeling of love for the city.

More than a look or visual impression, city style is a simple way of
life and an attitude that can be applied to every aspect of city living
and the urban home. It is about striking that balance between the
demands of urban living and our own personal well-being. It is
about achieving comfort, joy, and a sense of calm in our homes in
the heart of the city. When traveling for business and pleasure
throughout Africa and Europe, I look forward most to exploring a
new city and meeting its people. Browsing the marketplaces, shop-
ping with the locals, or dining with family tells me all I need to know
about a city. From my travels I have come to realize that although
cities may have distinctively different traditions and histories and
are perhaps at different ends of the economic spectrum, in many
ways their inhabitants have much in common, and these similari-
ties are the core of city style.

OPPOSITE

The familial nature of town houses brings a human scale and quality to the urban landscape that easily bridges the connection from one century to the next.

RIGHT

With attention to simplicity, this dining space in Hong Kong whispers serenity.

In strong contrast to the egocentric era of the 1980s and early 1990s, when more of anything gave us gratification, we are now falling in love with the simple side of city life, slowing down a bit, and enjoying even the smallest pleasures that a city has to offer. This growing attraction for walkable cities and an active street scene—where film, cafés, parks, bookstores, gyms, corner stores, and other accessible destinations predominate—defines neighborhood spirit and city style. Along with the redefinition of our relationship to our metropolitan environment is a change in the concept of home. It has been said that, historically, the turn of every new century instills people with a sense of nostalgia. Although the 21st century has truly brought us into a new modern age, our hearts still belong to the last century. Nowhere is this dichotomy felt more keenly than in the cities around the world, where the concern for security and burgeoning population is balanced by the explosion of interest in history, old architecture, and the environmentally inspired small-town approach to community life. It is about rediscovering the simpler, hands-on approach to city living.

Since September 11, people are not as eager to live in the clouds. Many corporations see campus-like environments as desirable places to house their employees, and many employees opt to work from home. Today, we view interiors not only in terms of quantity or size also but quality. There is a demand for intelligent space that is designed not only to efficiently meet our daily needs and functional demands but also to support us in achieving comforts of all kinds. Even small apartments, which may require us to simplify, should not leave us with the feeling that something is missing.

From Tokyo to Vancouver, *City Living* will lead you on a global tour of urban apartments—from small flats, lofts, and studios to town houses, row houses, and mansions—featuring fresh designs and practical solutions for simplifying busy metropolitan lifestyles. From Asian high-tech supercities, such as Hong Kong, to classic yet fashionable cities on the water, such as Stockholm, urbanites will reveal design and decoration ideas as well as solutions for achieving privacy, relaxation, comfort, convenience, and spiritual well-being in the heart of the city.

The Joys of Multicultural City Neighborhoods

Urban communities—where the households reflect a blend of racial groups and nationalities, and a blend of social, economic, and mixed-age backgrounds—are eclectic and dynamic cities. From Asians, African Americans, and Hispanics to seniors and college students, mixed populations tend to be more comfortable and thrive in diverse city communities.

Restaurants and Ethnic Cuisine

One of the biggest advantages of the multicultural urban scene is the influence it has on popular culture and lifestyle, especially on the options for diet and cuisine. Ingredients can come from Europe, South America, or Indonesia. The wide variety of international restaurants and demand for global cuisine is not only introducing new foods to our daily diets but is also changing the urban landscape and reflecting the melting of diverse populations in cities around the world.

Ethnic and Open Markets

Markets that sell herbs, spices, fruits, and ingredients from around the world are growing in popularity. Foods, such as fish that are only common to warmer waters of the world, are now easily available to shoppers in cold-climate countries. Cooking ingredients such as rose water, generally added to Middle Eastern rice dishes, and turbinado sugar, made from Hawaiian sugar cane, once uncommon in the continental United States, are now available at ethnic and farmers' markets.

London has 62 outdoor markets, which offer everything from the freshest seasonal foods to vintage clothing and flea-market bric-a-brac. Shoppers at the Portobello Road market in the Notting Hill section of London have lots to choose from the tables, stalls, and shops throughout the neighborhood. Visiting this mix of everything from foods to antiques is an all-day adventure. Brixton market with its many

West Indian shops is another popular marketplace with great buys and a wonderful international feel.

Open-air markets such as the Ninth Street Italian Market in Philadelphia, America's largest working outdoor market, is made up of shops and open-air stalls, where the bustle of shoppers and the aromas of foods mix to create an old-world flavor. Shops that make their own pastas and breads, as well as restaurants and bookstores, spill over into small side streets. Located in the center of Stockholm, Hötorget market, which consists of both outdoor and indoor stalls, offers fresh fruits, produce, vegetables, breads, and flowers from exotic places. Many come to meet friends over a casual lunch, shop for hard-to-find food ingredients, or conveniently buy dinner on their way to the metro. Outdoor and farmers' markets are great places to shop for high-quality and exotic foods, and the bustle of activity and exotic fragrances and aromas gives these markets a unique urban ambience.

Convenience

The convenience of accessible shops and markets that you pass on your way to and from work or the gym gives metropolitan areas a small-town feeling. In large, impersonal cities, it is a comfort to have a familiar face providing service. Bakeries, bookstores, boutiques, and corner stores are the anchors of walkable cities. Creating relationships between residents and business and supporting those businesses goes a long way in stabilizing neighborhoods and maintaining those that are already thriving.

Outdoor Recreation

Not just popular meeting places and anchors of a neighborhood, green spaces—such as city parks, squares, and community gardens—are sometimes the only outdoor recreational space available to city dwellers, especially those who live in apartments. Young and old alike enjoy taking advantage of these green spaces for playing sports, walking pets, or just hanging out and people watching.

CHAPTER 1

ARCHITECTURE, THE FIRST IMPRESSION OF THE CITY

From its early beginnings, the city was always about the people and how to accommodate them. They came from rural villages and the countryside, looking for community and social life, convenient marketplaces to buy and sell, cultural freedom, education, and, most of all, safety.

Protected by massive stone walls, inhabitants of medieval European cities went to great measures to keep menacing elements at bay.

What is a city if not the people?

Despite patrols by the law, come nightfall, highway robbery and other crimes awaited anyone traveling outside the city limits. It wasn't long before clergy, merchants, educators, artisans, masons, and others left farming communities to make a living amid a growing population. Despite devastating disasters in cities around the world—the great fire of London in 1666, the near total destruction of Atlanta during the American Civil War, and the earthquakes in Tokyo and San Francisco—cities rebounded and were built anew by subsequent generations. In the life of a city, the years it takes to rebuild is but a fraction of time in a city's existence.

The luster of 21st-century city life continues to fascinate and lure us for the similar reasons that attracted past generations: convenience, cosmopolitan lifestyle, cultural attractions, a sense of community, great universities, and exciting jobs, all within historical settings. Such urban amenities found amid the beauty of historical architecture and within walking distance from home are considered a privilege. Whether blessed with ancient structures or characterized by glass-and-steel skyscrapers, a city's architectural style is the first impression it gives us. Homes, workplaces, cultural centers, and transportation systems chronicle a city's past and present. From the ornate art deco details of 1920s New York brownstones to Casablanca's pastel adobe house exteriors, architecture is the link to the history of the city and its people.

SPACE WITH ATTITUDE

The epitome of urban chic, city life doesn't get any better than the industrial buildings constructed in the 19th to the early 20th century. These buildings speak to our every sense of history as well as to the trend of grand living. Surrounded today by cafés, clubs, bookstores, and movie theaters, converted loft spaces are the crown jewels of big-city living. Usually located in the heart of the city, these former factories and warehouses were once workplaces for thousands of workers who produced everything from clothing to locomotives. In an age when manual and mechanical industries fueled not only city incomes but national economies as well, manufacturers were the force behind the machine age. Now, as standing testaments to a bygone industrial era,

these buildings have been reborn as today's ultimate urban-chic real estate—a little gritty, a little old-world-modern, and, unquestionably, a lot hip city style with history.

The luxury of voluminous spaces combined with generous sunlight is a blueprint for beautiful and unique interiors. But more than this, the inherent design and detail of these vintage machine-age spaces resonate an industrial energy, reflecting a former presence of handmade and machine productivity and creation, which distinguishes them from newer loft-like apartments. Features such as expansive skylights, cast-iron sliding partitions, and intricate networks of fire escapes—once practical solutions to accommodate hundreds of workers—are now the unique features that translate into true urban character. Add to this the personal history of what it was like for the mostly immigrant population to work in such places, and it is clear that although they may be inspirational for new open-plan living spaces, their energy, craftsmanship, and functional design can never be duplicated. More than urban treasures, the generous and unencumbered floor plans of industrial loft spaces extend an invitation or challenge to transform them into whatever we desire.

TOWN HOUSES AND ROW HOUSES

Whether historical, high-society digs or turn-of-the-century tenant workers' housing, town houses and row houses evoke a bit of the old-fashioned, old-world neighborhoods and tip the balance of city living in favor of a more human and familial quality.

From Chicago to Johannesburg, city houses built in a row were produced between the early 1600s and 1920s. Over the centuries, these town houses give

ABOVE

From the clean lines of modern furniture, the painted white brick-and-mortar walls, and the high gloss of natural wood floors, color, form, and texture have created a rich interpretation of minimalism.

LEFT

A temporary storage spot for a canoe reflects practical use of space on this 19th-century Philadelphia row house.

OPPOSITE

Row houses and town houses such as these quaint Boston residences make even the biggest of cities feel like a small town. The craftsmanship of hand-laid bricks, handmade shutters, ornamental wood columns, cobblestone walks, and cozy street lighting reflect a time when everything was lovingly produced by hand.

the city a human scale, circumvent the hectic pace, and add old-world character. New York brownstones, Philadelphia row houses, Stockholm *rad hus*, London town houses, Amsterdam separate houses, or New Orleans shotgun houses are some of the various city houses found around the world.

Nowhere else in metropolitan homes is city style more connected to the outdoor environment and at the same time so unpretentiously familial as in these houses all in a row. Whether lining narrow Philadelphia side streets or the banks of a canal in Amsterdam, row houses single-handedly transform the urban canvas into livable, domestic communi-

ties with a village quality. Even in the bustle of noisy automobiles and congestion, gracefully proportioned windows and beautifully detailed doors in a row evoke a kind of nostalgia, relaxing the hectic pace. Turrets, bay windows, porticos, boot scrapes, and busy-body mirrors are part of street scenarios. These old homes bring out the small town in every big city. Perhaps it is the love and care, that craftsmen of the past invested in each house, one brick at a time, that radiates a certain charm and compels us to stop and admire them. Today, those who are lucky enough to live in a center-city town house can appreciate the generous proportions that were originally designed for larger families with many more social activities. Large rooms were converted for parties and dinners, dining rooms and parlors were considered the home's major features, and guest rooms often had to accommodate visitors for months at a time. More than homes for the families, houses were also designed to accommodate live-in housekeepers and other employees. And in Amsterdam, the size of separate houses compensated for lack of actual warehouses to store shop goods, with the homes of merchants also featuring warehouse space on the top floor.

APARTMENTS, THE STAPLE OF CITY STYLE

Flats, cribs, pads, mansions—apartments are for anyone and everyone. In most large cities, there are more apartments than houses. From small efficiencies and one-room studios to penthouse apartments, our concept of space and how much we need varies from country to country and culture to culture. Some of us are used to sharing a small bedroom and gath

ering in a cozy living room to watch television with the family, but others grew up in big country kitchens and formal dining rooms. Whereas our comfort level is pretty much determined by our background, more practically, a city's population will also determine the size and design of apartments. Trends that enhance the quality of city living are transported

OPPOSITE

Older apartments often are the best spaces for modern and whimsical design. Ornate windows, decorative molding, and fireplace mantles invite color and pattern and set the stage for a wide range of style interpretations.

ABOVE LEFT

The attraction to living the high life is a global trend. From Kuala Lumpur to Miami, cities are moving up. Amid many other high-rise apartment buildings and overlooking the main arteries of the city, this Miami apartment maintains a feeling of connectedness.

ABOVE RIGHT

In the center of Miami, this intimate and warmly designed apartment is located in one of many high-rise apartment dwellings. More than views of waterways and evening city lights, the attraction of such apartments lies in the convenience and accessibility to everyday city life.

quickly and adopted easily all over the world, thanks to the information age. The appreciation for trees and parks, bright sunlit apartments with great views, terraces, balconies, and sun decks are becoming standard requests from potential owners. More than a large, four-sided concrete block, the new generation of apartment buildings has a softer look. They feature floor-to-ceiling glass, inviting as much sunlight as possible, and are very different in size and layout, some with double height. The market for apartments has become extremely responsive to the demands of urbanites. Materials like granite and slate in kitchens and bamboo floors are special features that reflect the trend toward luxury and comfort.

In a modern industrial country such as Japan, where the population is more than 100 million, the steady migration to large cities like Tokyo and Osaka has created a demand for apartments that often exceeds the supply. Even small apartments can be extremely pricey, depending on proximity to transportation, views, sunlight, and section of town—all factors that determine rent value. Such small apartments in Japan have ironically been dubbed mansions. With the city undergoing a construction boom during recent years, hundreds of small apartment complexes, most about eight stories, are being built throughout Tokyo. Breaking away from the traditional cramped and unembellished small spaces, today's city apartments are promoted as warm and relaxed environments. Attention to detail and imaginative use of space and materials in these new complexes are addressing the universal demands of city dwellers. Comfort and modern conveniences are sought-after key amenities. Apartment dwellers in Tokyo, as well as in Miami and London, are placing a high value on the luxury of walking to work or to the nearest subway and close proximity to day-care centers, parks, and other outdoor recreational spaces.

LIVING THE HIGH LIFE

New York, Hong Kong, and Kuala Lumpur are among the leaders when it comes to high-rise apartment buildings. But the attitude toward living in the clouds is changing in many cities around the world. In cities like London, where the comfort level was more conservative when it came to skyscrapers, many are now viewing high-rise apartment living as a sophisticated and appealing option. In Tokyo, there is also a growing demand for high-rise apartment buildings, which are being built at a feverish pitch. Despite their cold exteriors, some high-rise apartment buildings offer their residents a personal approach to urban life by making available services such as around-the-clock nurse service and free spas that feature free breakfast. This global attraction to ease and comfort as a way of balancing the frantic pace of the city is a global trend that can be felt inside and outside the home.

Small nooks and corners, odd angles, and unexpected spaces add to the design possibilities that evoke comfort and a sense of joy.

The glass-and-steel staircase conveys the new life of this 19th-century, yet quite modern, row house. Glass-and-steel-framed panels create an openness throughout the entire building. The staircase backdrop—a textured, Venetian-red painted wall, which extends from the first to the fourth floor—personalizes this ultra-modern design and aesthetically links all four floors.

Modernizing and Upgrading Older Structures

Although their prime locations have much to do with the skyrocketing value of older urban structures, the care and attention paid to architectural detail, craftsmanship, and structural strength are what render them unrivaled by today's building standards. They represent a time when construction was a craft and craftsmen took pride in the smallest details. Although many features—such as elaborate hand-laid brick and other masonry work, decorative parquet floors, leaded glass, and built-in cabinets—continue to entice us with their old-world charm, 21st-century home comforts and conveniences make upgrades and alterations just as desirable.

What to Change and What to Retain?

Updating older structures should begin with the indispensable, must-do, behind-the-scenes alterations that add to a home's quality of life, comfort level, and convenience. Because they address the building's infrastructure, many of these alterations are costly, requiring professional builders and technicians. All the same, these basic upgrades are considered safeguards that preserve a building against the ravages of time. For example, replacing old roofs, sealing and insulating walls and attics, updating electrical sys-

LEFT

The owners, intrepid mountaineers who enjoy rock climbing, wanted the space to be exciting as you climb the stairs, with dramatic views up and down through structural glass floors. Glass floor panels were incorporated to allow light to filter through to the four floors, adding to the feeling of openness throughout the home and allowing direct exposure to the interiors above and below. The four balconies located on each floor are not only a practical approach to adding more living space but also a relaxed way to incorporate the element of nature. Floor-to-ceiling glass to the rear of the home opens onto a beautiful view of a weeping willow tree.

tems, and modernizing plumbing, heating, and ventilation systems are alterations necessary to adapt an older structure to the latest energy-efficient equipment and computer capabilities.

Modernizing Older Building Begins with the Basics

ELECTRICAL UPGRADES

Because today's homes are equipped with many more electrical appliances and services than they were designed for, from washers and dryers and hot water tanks to telecommuting technology, electrical upgrades—for indoors and outdoors—are mandatory to support the added power usage.

KITCHEN APPLIANCES AND GADGETS

Espresso makers, mixers, juicers, convection ovens, freezers, and wine coolers all need sufficient power to function. From the quantity and the type of appliances used, a professional electrician can determine how much power your home will need.

UPGRADING HEATING AND VENTILATION SYSTEMS

The latest technology in home central-heating systems focuses on green technology, lower fuel consumption, and lower cost. The EPA says that indoor air is 70 times more polluted than outdoor air. With that in mind, these new energy- and space-saving gas, oil, and electric

ABOVE

The kitchen's generous opening onto a Japanese Zen-inspired garden creates a fresh and open feeling. The custom-built dining table with casters makes al fresco dining and entertaining outdoors a simple transition.

systems do much to make a home clean, healthy, and comfortable. The heat is distributed more evenly throughout, at a faster rate and with minimal emissions, long-term corrosion of radiators and pipes is eliminated. Older homes were usually outfitted with a boiler. Most homes today, however, have furnaces and heat pumps that warm the air before it is circulated.

Whereas most urban homes in the United States are heated by natural gas, oil, or electricity, in Europe other modern forms of heating technology, such as radiant heating, have been popular for decades. Radiant heat involves the circulation of heated water, heated by gas, electricity, or solar power, through flexible tubing just below the surface of the floor, walls, or ceilings.

PLUMBING

Plumbing upgrades include everything from accommodating radiant heating and air-conditioning to septic and sprinkler systems.

As with new heating systems, upgraded plumbing networks focus on water conservation and efficiency. Replacing cast-iron pipes with PVC preserves the system in place. PVC can be somewhat noisy behind the walls when you flush the toilet, but insulating the pipes helps.

INSULATION AND WEATHERIZATION

Insulating and sealing doors and windows are basic climate-control procedures that can help make a home feel more comfortable. No matter how efficient your heating system is, if the construction is not tight and walls, doors, and windows allow heat to escape and cold air to seep in, you're wasting fuel and money. Homes that are drafty and poorly insulated will never feel comfortable during the winter months.

STRUCTURAL UPGRADES AND SPACE ALTERATIONS

The changes to older structures that we notice first are the architectural renovations that affect traffic flow and layout. Alterations can include modernizing staircases, removing wall partitions and narrow corridors, raising ceilings, and

OPPOSITE

The combination of steel cabinets, marble countertops, and metal-faced appliances, along with the original wide-board floors and textured window glass, is a comfortable contrast and union of original architectural features and modern design.

RIGHT

Space and storage, always a concern in narrow row homes, is addressed in this bedroom design solution. The floor-to-ceiling mirrored wall surface alters the character and maximizes the spatial perception, making the room feel larger. In addition, the separate dressing room outfitted with built-in shelving compartments provides much needed storage, space often unavailable in older city homes.

introducing new building materials and finishes that add interesting and contrasting influences. Some alterations that maximize space and make a room feel airy and open follow:

- Glass partitions and glass floors redirect light and allow it to brighten areas of four- or five-story town houses that are usually illuminated with electric lighting.

- When enlarging windows and adding glass doors, the more you see of the outdoors, the more spacious an area feels. The expansive outdoor view, not the dimensions of the room, becomes the focus.

- Walls with light-colored or high-gloss paint or flooring with a polished finish help reflect light, making the room feel more open.

- If lack of space is a major concern, replacing old stairways with more minimal versions physically frees up space and adds clean sim-

plicity to the total structure. Opening up stairwells, by removing walls around them and closet storage space below them, gives a home lots of breathing space. However, such a major renovation certainly alters the traditional character of an older town house and gives it a contemporary look.

- Adding on outdoor balconies, decks, and terraces to narrow row houses and town houses provides optional living space. During the warmer months in cold-climate cities and year-round elsewhere, these additions become extra rooms used for dining, entertaining, relaxing, or even working.

- Eventually, the lighting in 19th-and 20th-century city row houses has to be upgraded, for practical as well as aesthetic reasons. Hiring a professional electrician—and opening walls and ceilings—makes lighting installation an expensive upgrade. In the long term, however, it is well worth the cost. Such a

The fact that the building was not structurally sound and the interior structure needed to be removed and rebuilt allowed the owner and architect to consider the interior from scratch. The modernization of this 19th-century row house begins with the entrance. A floor-to-ceiling glass-and-steel panel softens the transition from the outdoors as you enter the spacious first floor. Once inside, the removal of room partitions created a generous open space.

change will affect the overall character of the home. Whether energy-efficient halogen recessed lighting, intimate incandescent wall sconces, or long-lasting compact fluorescent fixtures are desired, lighting should be considered in the early stages of renovation, when wiring and installation within walls and ceilings is easiest.

- Modernizing kitchens and bathrooms easily increases the value of your home. Stylish professional appliances and equipment, designer cabinets, clever storage spaces, and unique wall and floor finishes can alter the character of a kitchen and give it a contemporary feel. Because of the industrial character that appliances and gadgets have, kitchens can present the easy blend of modern and traditional elements. From original wide-board wooden floors and leaded glass windows to stainless-steel cabinets and professional-grade appliances, such combinations of old and new retain the soul of a structure.

The owners asked their architect, Colin Flavin, to address the negative features of row houses, such as the lack of natural light and access to a garden space. His solution was four cantilevered balconies at the rear of the house that invite light and nature into the structure and provide convenient access to additional outdoor living space.

Personalizing Entryways

Some of the most charming cityscapes are streets lined with row homes, adorned with front yards, curbside gardens, window boxes, and trees. Although brownstones, town houses, row houses, and small apartment buildings have similar architecture and were originally designed for a consistent look and feel, it is the unique personality of their owners that gives identical row homes a distinctively individual character.

Without porches, walkways, or front gardens to soften the transition from street to indoors and to distinguish each home, their exterior facades would seem like one big structure.

Window Boxes

Window boxes brimming with plants and flowers of the season add charm and liven up an entrance. They are the easiest, most effective way of turning a house into a home and conveying the feeling that someone who cares lives there. The visual impact of vibrant colors against neutral building materials has a striking effect. Even the most standard of windows takes on a special quality when adorned with a box full of colorful geraniums.

Pots and Containers

Even without a front yard, you can create a garden effect by placing three to five flowerpots of various sizes on front steps, landings, and stoops. It will soften the appearance of your urban entrance and create a warm, welcoming first impression. Flowers symmetrically placed on either side of the front stairs or door create a more formal welcome.

Curbside Gardens

Grassy curbside spaces, along the edge of the sidewalk where trees and flowers can be planted, create a small-town ambience for homes in the biggest of cities. Trees and flowerbeds that line the pavement often provide the only outdoor green space for apartment dwellers. Low-maintenance ornamental grasses and annuals and perennials add joyful splashes of color, enriching a home's exterior.

The Front Door

A freshly painted front door makes a wonderful greeting. Make sure the windows are clean and the street number is clear and easy to read. The beauty and craftsmanship of front doors are often hidden under a single coat of paint—a

second, contrasting hue can bring out unique architectural features and details such as doorbells, door knockers, and knobs. Depending on the choice of colors, highlighting panels and windows can add an element of elegance or whimsy.

Seasonal Wreaths

Seasonal wreaths are one way to celebrate the change of seasons and holidays and to personalize your front door. Decorate with boxwood and pine branches, or with fresh herbs, such as rosemary and thyme, for fragrance. Colorful fall leaves and raffia will add a not-so-fussy casual look to fall and winter displays.

Porches

Both a living and greeting space, porches are a sunny place to sit with coffee and the morning paper, take a nap, or casually greet company.

During the warm weather, porches become outdoor rooms. Easily cleaned furnishings, plants and flowers, and outdoor lights and lanterns can turn porches into outdoor rooms

Lighting

A porch light, a small lamp mounted next to or over the door entrance, indoor lighting that pours through door windows, or ground-level lighting for shrubs and trees can produce dramatic or homey visual impressions. Of course, outdoor lighting serves the functional purpose of providing light to find keys, to read addresses, and so on. However, the warm glow of incandescent lighting emotionally and aesthetically frames an entrance of architectural details, plants, flowers, beautiful door knockers, and other accessories. Leaving the outdoor nightlight burning is one sure way to evoke a sense of home for an entrance.

CHAPTER 2

THE ILLUSION OF SPACE

As with any other diminishing resource, city dwellers place a high value on living space. Although it is not really decreasing, population spurts and development sprawl make it feel as if it is. Despite a drop in population in some large cities, the demand is still high for space in the neighborhoods and districts considered most fashionable. Even areas outside of cities, where square footage and acreage command a high premium, see escalating value, which will only increase in the future. Space is becoming a true luxury.

So what is it that we find so desirable about having lots of space, often more space than we can functionally use? Perhaps, it is just the status and prestige of being able to afford a big house. Maybe it is the insular feeling of privacy that distant proximity from neighbors can foster. How about the old adage "bigger is better"? Or could it be that we actually need all those rooms? It all comes down to how we define our lives and the concept of home. City style is all about using what you have and creatively and resourcefully meeting the needs of your family.

OPPOSITE

From the modest use of space to the floor seating, this intimate dining area captures the essence of Japanese culture and visually expresses their minimal approach to design.

LEFT

Grand comfort has been achieved without sacrifice in this very small space. This cozy bedroom offers enough space to have everything you need just within reach.

USING THE SPACE THAT YOU HAVE

Many people associate and equate quality of life with big real estate. However, everything is relative, and as city populations grow and apartments become more compact, we have learned that you do not have to sacrifice quality of life in small-space living. Quite the contrary, megacities such as Kuala Lumpur, New York, Tokyo, and Paris, where apartments can be very small, also boast the world's most fashionable, comfortable, and expensive apartments and houses.

"Oh, we never use that room."

Whether you are converting a large, open-plan space to a cozy interior, downsizing your life to fit a studio apartment, or adapting an 18th-century row house to an expanding 20th-century family, space is an issue. The "city" approach to space is about function, creativity, resourcefulness, and spirit. It is not about having more and more space but rather using the space that you have in a clever and thoughtful way that can result in comforts of all kinds—physical, emotional, and spiritual.

TOO MUCH SPACE?

Lofts and Other "Living Large" Spaces

Whereas the beauty of loft living has much to do with great center-city locations, 16-foot (4.9 m) ceilings, and fabulous windows that bring panoramic city views indoors, the lure of such spacious and unstructured interiors ultimately lies in their enormous design possibilities. Subdividing and reconfiguring large spaces into comfortable and multifunctional living areas are creative challenges, ones that provide the opportunity for us to reevaluate our priorities

Like no other, unstructured spaces offer the opportunity to make the space our own.

and visually express what gives us joy. You get to decide where to place walls and how large to make the bedrooms. And, if you prefer to dine and entertain in the kitchen, you don't have to have a dining room at all.

Personalizing such a large square footage requires an organizational plan, without which industrial spaces could be a bit overwhelming. To enter a loft space and see all four walls and everything in between in one glance leaves little to explore and takes away the element of the unexpected. The lure

Perfect for one room or loft-space living, this glass panel not only adds character but also effectively divides the bedroom from the bath without distracting from the spacious and airy quality of the interior.

of what lies around the corner in the next room is as important for a large single space as it is for more traditional layouts, even if the corner consists of only a standing screen, a fabric panel, or another improvisational room divider. Once the overall architectural features, such as windows, doors, trims, floors, and hardware finishes, are uniform throughout, interior spaces can be subdivided without fear of losing the character of the original space.

Divide and Conquer

One way to convert voluminous one-space industrial lofts into functional and, ultimately, intimate living interiors is by reconfiguring and dividing the space. This can be done in several ways.

- **Walls and Permanent Partitions** Constructing a fixed metal, wood, plaster, or drywall partition that extends from floor to ceiling is the most

As demonstrated here, furniture and function are often the ideal room dividers. Through the use of contrasting styles and textures, the living spaces of this large single space accommodate dining, socializing, and food preparation without the use of partitions.

expensive and permanent solution for altering large single spaces and usually requires the planning of an interior designer or architect. However, this solution guarantees the greatest amount of privacy and long-term use, which is especially necessary for bathrooms and bedrooms. Aside from providing permanently defined interior spaces, wall partitions can be painted, decorated with hanging art or cutouts, or embellished in ways that are limited only by the imagination. Because you are effectively creating a large apartment, the disadvantage is that you may partially compromise the airy character of the loft and the signature lighting schemes.

- **Glass Partitions** Frosted, tinted, ribbed, embossed, or glass block partitions have become staples in contemporary urban interiors. Over the years, glass block, in particular, has been a popular design option for both aesthetic and security reasons. For exterior walls, it allows light to filter in and at the same time provides the strength of an outer wall. The advantage of using interior glass partitions is you establish the functional boundaries of a room while maintaining the overall spacious quality, allowing natural light to filter

through in beautiful ways. How the light is diffused depends on the kind of glass you use.

- **Freestanding Screens and Panels** Freestanding panels or folding screens are a more flexible solution for improvisational spaces and can be moved and rearranged at will. They are perfect for work-at-home spaces or for providing instant privacy for guests. Whether produced from plywood, particleboard, fabric, or natural fibers, they do the job of visually breaking up the space. Sheer-colored textiles, extended from ceiling to floor, are softer, more dramatic partitions that retain the ambience of voluminous light and space while establishing room boundaries.

- **Carpets** If privacy is not an issue, carpets can be excellent room dividers, depending on how the space is used. They serve three general functions. First, they set perimeters and define room boundaries in a simple way. Next, they aesthetically connect all of the furnishings, creating a unified sense of function for the furnishings. Lastly, carpets stabilize and help to anchor a room setting, eliminating the illusion of floating, unconnected furniture.

- **Furniture** Furniture can act as an improvisational form of room divider while also being a part of the furniture grouping. From credenzas to open shelves and from storage units to sofas, furniture is a contemporary solution to dividing space. Just remember that the backside of these furnishings will also be visible.

TOO LITTLE SPACE

No matter how large or small rooms may appear, as soon as furniture is added to the space, the dimensions seem to change. Therefore, if size is an issue and your goal is to visually expand your space, function and purpose should be a priority when choosing furniture. Smaller room proportions do not mean you have to sacrifice comfort or beauty; just simplify your choices. Choosing the right furnishings for a narrow Philadelphia row house or tiny Tokyo apartment can help achieve a roomier atmosphere.

Uncomplicated city homes provide for a relaxed city lifestyle.

The key to furnishing small spaces is to simplify.

- Think about the function and purpose of the small room. These aspects of the room will guide you in simplifying the quantity, style, and placement of furniture.

- Flexible chairs, tables, and cabinetry that fold, stack, hang, or roll can easily solve the problem of too much demand on too little space. Bring pieces out only when needed.

- Multifunctional and double-duty furniture—such as coffee tables that raise and expand into dining tables, beds that have bases designed for storage, and decorative cabinets that open to reveal homework stations—can help make a space more versatile.

Tones of beige and white, simple lines, lots of sunlight, and mirrored wall make this bedroom feel larger than it really is.

Despite the tropical and rich, dark woods, this room feels warm and inviting because of the abundance of sunlight.

Creating the Illusion of More Space with Furniture

- Keep furniture finishes the same throughout a room. It is less distracting and allows the eye to take in the whole space.

- Keep upholstery fabrics discreet, with simple patterns. Save the unique motifs and patterns for smaller accent chairs and stools.

- Choose wood- or metal-framed sofas and chairs without skirts or flaps, as opposed to heavy, upholstered pieces, for a slimmer look. Their exposed legs visually separate them from the floor, giving the furniture and the area around them a lighter impression.

- Keep seating, beds, and cabinetry low to create an airy ambience at eye-level height.

- Aim for soft curves, restrained decorative details, and simple, classic lines, as these easily coexist within interior space.

- Add a sense of light with glass-top tables and glossy surfaces, from counters to floors.

- In tiny spaces, keep seating and storage furnishings close to the wall. If possible, attach shelving directly to walls.

Visually Expand a Space with Color, Mirrors, and Light

- **Color and Paint** To visually expand your space, paint walls white or other soft colors. These hues will reflect, not absorb, natural sunlight. Light-colored floors also bounce the light and make a room bright and airy, especially those with high-gloss finishes.

- **Mirrors** Light can be reflected and space can be visually expanded in a room by using mirrors. When positioned to face the light source, mirrors become a source of light themselves, making the room brighter. From the living room to the kitchen, mirrors are beautiful when casually leaning against a wall or set as reflective backsplashes, tucked between kitchen countertops and wall cabinets. Both applications aesthetically and functionally create a feeling of more space.

- **Natural Light** Sunlight and moonlight that pours in through overhead skylights change the general feeling of the space, washing evenly over a room and creating a cheerful and calming atmosphere.

The combination of lots of natural light, reflective surfaces, and soft, contrasting colors comes together to increase our sense of space in this London apartment. The ultimate luxury here is not expensive furnishings, but beautifully framed, tranquil space with a touch of drama and whimsy.

JUST ENOUGH SPACE, AND BABY MAKES THREE

The need for more space is a primary incentive when looking for a new home. We look for just the right amount of space to meet our family's needs. However, once we are in the new home with just the right amount of space, with more room for entertaining friends, more comfort zones, and a bigger kitchen, it doesn't take long before the right amount of space starts to shrink. A new baby comes, we decide to work at home, or the clutter begins to take over, and before you know it, what used to be perfect is no longer enough.

Some Solutions

- **Organization and Clever Storage** Personal items, such as clothing, magazines, furniture, and books, are easy to accumulate and hard to part with. Storing clothes with the hope that they will come back into style is not as essential as, say, saving clothes for younger children. Organization is about knowing what is necessary and what you can do without. Let's face it: Some things will not come back into style. One way to determine what should be saved is to ask yourself, "When was the last time I used this?" "When will I use it again?" and "Could someone else have a greater appreciation for it?" Hold onto your favorites, and let the others go. Remember that simplicity is the key. To keep the balance of just enough space, we should always be aware of accumulating possessions.

- **Double-Duty Rooms** Dining rooms are commonly the first to do double duty, converting to office space, family room, or library. Futons, trundles, and sofa beds multiply the capacity for guests and allow rooms to resume their original purposes when guests have gone. Dining tables that double as a work surface and decorative cabinets that can hold computers, printers, or other office equipment are effective solutions for maintaining the "just enough space" status of a room.

- **Outside Spaces: The New Living Rooms** Reconsider rooftops and balconies. No longer valued only as extra square footage, these outer zones have added a new dimension to urban living and created opportunities to connect daily to the natural environment and enjoy the outdoors. Taking our cue from the Japanese, Dutch, and English passion for gardening and the integration of indoor and outdoor living spaces, Americans have expressed a growing enthusiasm for private and community gardens in their cities.

  Urbanites are spending more time working in and enjoying their gardens and redefining their outside rooms. Even the smallest outdoor space offers an opportunity to extend our living into the outdoors, whether for dining in the garden or napping on the balcony.

The organic and fluid forms of this Japanese city home take the edge off of urban living and reflect a loving relationship with nature. A sliding floor-to-ceiling glass panel renders the indoors and outdoors indistinguishable. Curbside trees and shrubs add to the spiritual element of nature.

Neutral tones, lots of sunlight, simple lines, and generous windows evoke the illusion of space.

The Illusion of Space

Most city homes are not designed with generous storage space, and the older they are, the less there is. Add to that the normal accumulation that occurs over the years, and before you know it, we are overrun with clutter. It just happens. For practical or emotional reasons, it can be hard to part with things, but sooner or later we have to decide what is worth saving and what we can do without. Before thinking of the trash bin, there are a number of options, such as fund-raising thrift stores, yard sales, flea markets, or friends and family.

For those things you can't live without, there is storage. Organization has a major effect on how our homes look and feel, so before the clutter becomes overwhelming, make storage as much a priority as decorating. Today there are stylish, clever, and affordable solutions for everything from dressing closets to recycle bins. Excessive clutter and lack of organization is not only a waste of space but also a waste of our time and energy. Storage and organization is big business, and companies have become responsive to the needs of small-space living and clever storage packaging.

Everyday versus Long-Term Storage
Items used every day should be close at hand with easy access. Using attractive baskets, cubbies, and bins to store newspaper, toys, clothing, or cleaning agents saves space as well as time and energy, all of which adds a degree of comfort to our home. On the other hand, items that are needed seasonally and require long-term storage, such as gardening tools and accessories, holiday decorations, and seasonal clothing, can be relegated to the basement, attic, or out-of-reach storage.

Walls
Bookcases, shelving, and built-in cabinetry are the easiest, most assessable kinds of storage. Well-proportioned wall systems store stereo equipment, the TV, books, bar supplies, food, and all manner of collections efficiently. They can accommodate padded boards, hooks to hang things, kitchen utensils, and so on.

Easy and Simple

Large woven African baskets become beautiful hampers for the bath and bedroom or toy storage containers for the living room. Plastic bins stationed in the mudroom are convenient drop-off points for hats, scarves, and gloves. Small tins or baskets that can be removed and placed quickly on shelves are great for kitchen utensils. Storage units and cupboards with castors offer much-needed storage and flexibility. Covered boxes that can slide under the bed, as well as canvas racks that hang in closets, conveniently hold shoes, folded clothing, and accessories.

Portable

Trolleys, carts, bins, and drawer units on casters are stylish, flexible solutions for accessible storage wherever they are needed. Perfect for storing kitchen, bathroom, living room, or home office items, they can be made of metal, wood, or heavy canvas.

Built In and Concealed

Sometimes storage is the perfect solution for organizational needs, but in the process, it becomes a major distraction. By completely or partially concealing shelves, cabinets, and bookcases with doors and fabrics, the distraction can often be hidden. Concealed storage under staircases, below window seats, or built-in closets that are seamless with walls not only hides the contents but can also camouflages the fact that the storage exists.

Tables

Coffee tables designed as chests or those with drawers double as storage places. Nesting tables and stools that conveniently slide under each other or stack are the perfect space-saving solutions. Although small city apartments may not be able to accommodate a side table for every chair, stackable tables are practical solutions for special occasions.

Chairs

In the bedroom, chairs and ottomans can be placed beside the bed for additional surface storage instead of small tables. No home should be without folding chairs the classic space saver. They can be stored on hooks on a wall until extra seating is needed for parties and gatherings. Stackable chairs are a must for any city home, with the plastic indoor/outdoor chairs being replaced with ones now produced by designers such as Phillip Stark.

Storage with a Focus on Design

When storage solutions are a major feature or focal point of a room, the decorative style must consistently work with the other furnishings and architectural in the room. Whether it is a 19th-century armoire used to hold stereo equipment and CDs in a traditional or formal interior or simple floor-to-ceiling bookcases or glass shelves for display and storage for a minimalist look, make sure the design style is not sacrificed for the practical purpose of storage.

Decorative Storage

Vintage trunks and chests double as unique accent furniture and practical storage solutions. Elegant hat boxes, woven baskets that hold everything from rolls of toilet paper to rolled towels, and hand-carved boxes for jewelry and hair assessories are practical storage areas as well as decorative elements in a room.

A certain comfort exists in the minimal, pared-down look and feel of this redesigned London town house. The comfort of knowing that everything is in its place with no clutter to primp and maintain lends comfort and piece of mind. For those who appreciate the Zen-like surroundings of uncompli-cated space, a simple color palette, easy access to the garden, and comfortable bed rest, this will be a place of well-being in the heart of downtown.

CHAPTER 3

CITY COMFORTS

The world's largest cities, such as New York, Paris, London, and Tokyo, with populations upward of 14 million, exemplify the phrase "the city that never sleeps." In these cities, the streets are often as bustling at midnight as they are at noon. Stores are open and services are available around the clock. We're so used to traffic gridlock that we take along music or something to read for the wait. Waiting in check-out lines at the supermarket and listening to Muzak while on hold have become a way of life. Inevitably, because of the hectic pace of city living, we are constantly in the company of others. It is small wonder that our homes have become sweeter than ever. More and more they are seen as the one place where we truly feel secure, where life becomes man-ageable and calm, and, to some degree, where we have control over our busy world.

Finding tranquility in the cities that never sleep.

Calm, muted colors, organic textures, furniture from traditional cultures, and a symmetrical layout create a relaxed environment but with a somewhat formal approach. The fine balance of all these elements evokes a Zen-like quality that can be adapted to city homes around the world.

COMFORTS OF ALL KINDS

The dictionary offers several definitions for the term "comfort." One meaning that sums it up best defines it as "a state of ease and satisfaction of bodily wants, with freedom from pain and anxiety." This definition speaks not only to physical anxieties, but also to mental and emotional ones—the stress of life. In fact, this more holistic view of comfort is the catalyst for much of our changing attitude concerning 21st-century home and lifestyle. From comfort foods to soothing colors, it is all aimed at creating environments that are calm and free from anxiety. As we navigate our urban lives through these unpredictable and often-turbulent times, many of us suffer adverse physical, emotional, and spiritual side effects. Stress-related medical conditions, such as heart attacks, ulcers, high blood pressure, and depression, plague us and have prompted many of us to seek a more introspective and spiritual home atmosphere and lifestyle. The pursuit of relaxation and quality of life is a high priority, especially for urbanites. The more we learn about the causes of stress, the more we understand how our immediate home environment can affect the balance of that equation. Indeed, for most of us, home is the place where we can achieve unconditional comfort, from the furnishings we choose to the food we eat to the company we keep. Home is where we strive to achieve physical, emotional, and spiritual comforts and balance the adverse effects of 21st-century urban life.

Some may consider sleeping in on Sunday mornings and awaking to a jumbo Sunday newspaper and a small stack of pancakes as the ultimate in relaxation. In our hectic lives, the significance of leisure time and the ability to spend that time doing whatever we choose is a true luxury. Often, we do not think of the element of time when decorating our homes. However, it is one of the ingredients that inspires the look and feel of a home. It really shows when we do not have time for ourselves or our surroundings. Clutter and disarray express a lack of loving care for a home. And where there is lack of care, there can be very little comfort. The decorating and lifestyle mantra of our time—"Surround yourself with the things you love"—could never be more applicable. Therefore, before designing and furnishing our homes, we must carefully think through what gives us the greatest degree of comfort and joy and how we will relax, unwind, and find solace in our environment.

THE ELEMENTS OF A COMFORTABLE HOME

Physical Comforts

Physical comfort is more than big, fluffy beds and cushy sofas. Not everyone likes mountains of pillows or soft mattresses. Furniture should be easy, simply allowing the body to relax without restrictions and a lot of fuss. Rest your feet, curl up, and recline. After all, if we can't indulge ourselves at home, where else can we? As long as the upholstery is stain resistant and we give it a modicum of respect, why not enjoy? The concept of comfort is subjective and completely different for each of us. Nevertheless, creating it still requires that practical design guidelines be followed and emotional and spiritual factors be considered. A level of comfort comes from interiors that are organized and well thought out. A comfortable space needs to be outfitted with reliable furniture and storage. When rooms are laid out logically and furniture is positioned appropriately, communication is enhanced, views are uninterrupted, and the appreciation that things are where they should be gives us a sense of relaxation. We don't often think of organization and symmetry as things that provide comfort, but confidence in the good design of a space is quite reassuring.

Furniture

Is it better to look good or feel good? When selecting furniture with comfort as a priority, design, function, and quality of craftsmanship should be your first considerations. If these three criteria are not met, that beautiful chair or sofa will ultimately be avoided, no matter where they are placed or how beautiful they look.

- **Design** A beautiful, sumptuous-looking sofa with decorative pillows and bolsters that leave little room to sit may not be as restful as it looks. Often the most comfortable furniture is the most simple in terms of lines and form. Uncomplicated lines and gentle curves, balanced proportions, relaxing seat cushions, and soft upholstery are the four furniture ingredients that define a relaxed yet luxurious style. Embellishment and decoration can add beauty to a furniture piece that is designed with care, but be aware of excesses that compromise true comfort.

- **Craftsmanship** A good seat should not only support your weight but also allow for easy movement and change of positioning. Seat cushions can be constructed with springs, foam, feather, or other filling, depending on how soft or firm you want the seat to be. Most furniture is made by machine to ensure not only a certain level of production quality but also uniformity. Try the furniture out, and talk with the salesperson about the materials and construction of the piece as well as the warranties.

Furniture produced by hand in many countries around the world can offer exquisite craftsmanship that comes from the personal attention of the craftsman, as well as a one-of-a-kind look.

OPPOSITE

We all deserve a place to lean back and rest our feet at the end of the day. In this Moroccan courtyard retreat, surrounded by comfy seating, traditional colors and patterns, and lush plants and flowers, relaxation comes easy.

- **Proportion** The height of the seat back, the depth of the seat, and size of the arm are all important in determining physical comfort. Proper proportion will allow for comfortable movement and access. For example, the wraparound design and feel of a tuxedo sofa—featuring the back and arms at the same height—is beautiful, but it is not your kind of sofa if you like to recline while reading or watching TV.

- **Function** Every chair is not for lounging, nor does every chair have to have the maximum relaxation of an easy chair. It should, however, provide us with comfort to meet the function for which the furnishing was designed. For example, we can be more forgiving of dining room chairs, which are used for short periods. You're not expected to lounge, so they need not be as sumptuous as an easy chair. However, for those who entertain in more formal ways, an armchair may be perfect for lengthy dinner parties that go on into the evening.

Of course, furniture such as chaises and beds are in their own comfort category. It is estimated that the average person spends one-third of his or her life in bed, so it is understandable why everything from mattress firmness, pillow filling, and sheet thread count and quality can determine how comfortable our beds are.

ABOVE

Against the tranquil green backdrop of this intimate space in Singapore, finely crafted wood and woven rattan evoke relaxation and project a welcoming environment.

- **Placement** Creating balance with furniture placement is especially important. Because of the typically long and narrow layouts and smaller size of older row houses, town houses, and small apartments, furniture placement is pivotal. Living rooms generally serve multiple functions. They are rooms for entertaining guests, enjoying a video, gathering with the family, or just relaxing. It is important that the chairs, sofas, and tables relate and connect logically to each other and are grouped in settings that allow for relaxed conversation and socializing. Grouping furniture to allow for easy flow and access in and out of rooms is important to the balance of a room so as to avoid repeatedly maneuvering around or constantly moving the same piece of furniture.

- **Accent Furniture** Pieces such as benches, settees, stools, small tables, ottomans, and poufs all provide opportunities for extra comfort and are great for resting your feet or placing a glass, making life a little more leisurely. There is a kind of comfort in having an extra table within easy reach for the magazine or earphones, or a small stool beside the coffee table for the third person relegated to the middle of the three-seater sofa.

Emotional Comforts

Rooms at Rest There are many who believe that a certain kind of power emanates from a positive and loving environment, a force that balances the not-so-positive experiences of everyday life and ultimately helps us assert control over our own well-being. Whether by using inherited furnishings, souvenirs from travels, soothing music, or favorite colors, we have the power to influence our sense of emotional well-being. From a photograph, certain rooms visually and emotionally communicate a promise of serenity and evoke a restful and tranquil mood. Without trying out a sofa or testing a bed for physical comfort, we can connect with that quality. It could be the way sunlight catches the creases and folds of a down-feather sofa, a casual and intimate seating layout that accommodates relaxed conversation and socializing, or even the comfort that comes from being organized and knowing that things are in their proper place.

▪ **Period Styles, Vintage, and Antiques** It is no wonder that any attempt to recapture quieter, more peaceful times and associations have spawned a strong trend toward nostalgia. When translated into home decor, vintage or retro furniture and decoration allow us to experience bygone design periods with new appreciation. Heirlooms, antiques, and second-hand furniture and accessories have become pivotal elements in design. Portraits and other paintings and tabletop accessories, such as linens, lighting, and objects with personal meaning, all come together to create that spirit of the past and emotional comfort that is so appreciated for this age in which we live.

ABOVE

African-inspired interior design, and that of other traditional cultures, possesses a simple, almost minimal, quality. Restful earth colors that never go out of style, exotic natural fibers, and the imperfections of hand-forged accessories make the spiritual connection. Such interiors are perfect retreats for our city homes.

OPPOSITE

Founder and owner of Atlanta's Kubatana Gallery, Brian Wertz has created a serene and tranquil environment for both gallery space and home in which to present traditional and modern African and African-American art and design.

▪ **Comfort Colors** The most inexpensive way to express a room's character and mood is through the application of paint and color. Although some colors are considered more relaxing than others, how we relate to hues and tones is a subjective relationship. Each of us has created our own association to hues. A favorite dress, childhood memory, or the changing colors of fall can be inspiration for color choice.

Neutrals and monochromatic hues are not the only colors to enhance a sense of comfort. Cooler blues, greens, and lavender also fall into that restful category. Even muted reds, burnt orange, and ochre can evoke a sense of well-being. Color choices change from room to room. The color scheme of a relaxing living room can be completely different from that of a peaceful and intimate bedroom where rest is foremost. Walls, floors, upholstery, carpets, window fabrics, and accents all affect the emotional impact of color.

▪ **Personal Keepsakes, Memorabilia, and Collections**
What is a home without those pieces that define us and reaffirm who we are? From family photographs to favorite books and music, our homes are filled with such keepsakes that make the connection to our backgrounds and instinctively bring joy to our lives. It is important to keep personal treasures visible and a part of everyday use, not tucked away in a closet and used only for special occasions.

Rejuvenation and Relaxation

Today's perspective on good health no longer focuses solely on diet, exercise, and regular medical checkups, but rather it has taken a more holistic approach, one that includes the mind, body, spirit, and environment. Finding that balance in an increasingly complicated world is determined by how well we take care of ourselves. Time to relax, laugh, and enjoy healthy social relationships is as important as exercise and eating the right foods.

Young and old alike, we all require time to relax and rejuvenate and to rebound from everyday stresses. Whether we travel across town or across the Atlantic to come home, our personal living space is where we take time to heal and rejuvenate. That sense of calm and well-being can carry over to all aspects of our lives, from our relationships with others to our careers.

A Good Night's Sleep

No matter how young or old we are, it is so important to get a good night's rest. Often, long work hours, family responsibilities, studying for exams, or constant travel makes a good night's sleep impossible. A lack of sleep can affect concentration, memory, temperament, and reflexes, as well as influence job performance and social relationships. Sleep debt, as it is called, is something we sooner or later have to pay back, either by making up those lost hours of sleep or by poor physical and emotional performance. Each person's sleep quotient varies; no set number of hours is required for a good night's sleep. However, the true test is to awake rested.

Tips for getting a good night's sleep include:
- Try to get to bed at the same time every night.
- Don't nap during the day if you have a hard time sleeping at night.
- Avoid caffeine or smoking before sleeping because both caffeine and nicotine are stimulants.
- If you cannot sleep, get out of bed and do something relaxing, such as listening to soothing music or reading a favorite magazine.
- If you are tired early, just go to bed.
- Take a hot bath or shower to relax and prepare yourself for bed.
- Create a restful atmosphere with tranquil colors, candlelight, relaxing fragrances, soft lighting, soft music, comfy sheets, and a comfortable mattress to promote sound sleep.

The Bath

A soothing, warm bath does much to relax and relieve us from the stresses of the day. Hot tubs and Jacuzzis massage us with pressurized jets, but even standard tubs possess the traditional therapeutic power of water. Essential oils and organic bath salts added to the bath water, scented candles carefully placed, a variety of

Although modern and minimalist, pillow and cushion seating that is comfy and low to the floor takes its cue from ancient furniture design and creates a serene atmosphere.

plants and flowers, and soft lighting alter the atmosphere from a washing place to a spa dedicated to complete relaxation. Benefits of a hot bath include:

- Relaxation of tired muscles
- Increase in circulation
- Abatement of joint discomfort

Yoga

Yoga, a 5,000-year-old practice that originated in India's Hindu religion, has experienced an explosion of interest all over the world. Restorative to the mind and body, the goal of yoga is to improve physical and emotional health and to unite the mind and body as one.

Through breathing exercises, stretching and flexing muscles, chanting, assuming poses, and relaxing, many experience an overall sense of calm and well-being. Yoga promotes general good health and offers specific benefits, including:

- Lowered blood pressure
- Alleviation of chronic pain
- Lessened insomnia
- Decreased stress
- Increased muscle tone

Today, almost every gym offers a variety of yoga classes. However, once you have learned the fundamentals, you can practice in your own home. The best environment in which to practice yoga and meditation at home is in a quiet space, such as a bedroom or garden. You'll need enough floor space to assume the yoga poses. Additional considerations include relaxing light, such as candles, and soft music.

Prayer and Meditation

In a world of e-mail, cell phones, and PDAs, finding time for prayer or reflection is a challenge, but it provides a worthwhile contrast to how we spend the majority of the day. Prayer and meditation have filled the lives of the world's population since the dawn of religion, but it is now recognized for its positive influence on our physical state of health.

Regardless of one's particular faith, prayer reinforces the belief that we are not alone and that someone or something more powerful is guiding and supporting us. The spiritual nature of prayer and meditation helps us see our worries and concerns from a more positive perspective. Such belief is not only reassuring but emotionally empowering as well.

Prayer provides many benefits:
- It soothes our spiritual nature.
- It relaxes the body.
- It improves emotional health.

Home Altars

Once common in traditional cultures, home altars of various sorts are popular in households around the world. Often consisting of a collection of photographs, personal mementos, or favorite possessions, and sometimes adorned with candles, fresh herbs, or flowers, these symbolic areas remind us of and keep us connected to loved ones who have passed on. Altars can be created anywhere and only require enough space to carefully place and display your chosen items.

The interior design of this converted London town house makes a strong visual impact. The home's double-height windows and all-white walls boldly illuminate its interiors from the inside out. During the day, sunlight streams in to brighten the whole house from the outside in and creates a cheerful and uplifting environment.

CHAPTER 4

AN URBAN HOME IN EVERY SENSE

A home without attention paid to the sensory delights of everyday life is like an empty promise. No matter how beautifully a home is decorated, it falls miserably short without consideration to how it should be experienced through sight, touch, taste, smell, and sound. There is no secret to adding this element of joy and life to a home. Personal and subjective, we need only ask ourselves: What is it that gives us pleasure? Quite simply, each of us will have our own answer.

We have all been to homes that have an allure and inviting attraction, and for whatever reason, we feel welcome. It could be the fragrance of fresh-cut lilacs that meets you at the door, the glow of sunlight that washes over a room and speaks to our romantic side, or the feel of a toasty warm fire in the dead of winter. The delightful influence of color and light, fragrances and aromas that evoke fond associations, and textures that are soothing to the touch is pivotal in balancing out the frenzied and impersonal world outside our doors. In short, a home that excites our sense of vision, touch, taste, smell, and sound is as joyful as it is tantalizing.

VISUAL

The Beauty of Natural Light

Sunlight, and even moonlight, can have the most uplifting effect on our spirits. Cheerful yet calming, brilliant rays of sun filtering through windows have both a physical and emotional effect on our interior spaces, as well as on our own psyches. Unlike synthetic lighting, the glow of natural light adds a spiritual quality and makes a room feel larger than it is. Although the quality of light on overcast days is more pale and less bright, it can still have a flattering effect on furniture fabrics, carpets, and other accessories.

In northern cities, such as Stockholm, Oslo, or Helsinki, the appreciation for sunlight is more keenly felt than in cities to the south. From November to early February, the sun stays in the sky for only a few hours, so natural light is scarce. During these wintry months, the sun rises at about 10:00 A.M. and sets at 3:00 P.M., but candlelight and fireplaces are ablaze around the clock. The effect of softly flickering light casts a festive but serene ambience over a room. In Ghana, Nigeria, and other countries south of the Sahara desert, sunlight is interrupted once a year by the Harmattan. For a three-month-long dusty season that begins in late November or December, winds blow southward from the Sahara desert, with fine dust blocking the sun and making each day cloudy and overcast.

Because light—and the lack of it—can have such a tremendous effect on mood, it is important to use it to your advantage as much as possible. Plan the most popular and commonly used sitting and dining areas to receive the best light. If your home doesn't have many windows, expand and reflect the light you do get with mirrors, white and nearly white colors, and reflective surfaces. If possible, avoid furnishings or window treatments that hinder or block the flow of light.

The beauty of natural light is important to the visual impression of a home. It adds the sensual element of nature, creating shadows, highlights, and reflections on upholstery and finishes, as well as an emotional component that evokes an inviting and welcoming quality.

Color Choices

From the calming and restful effect of blues to the provocative and exciting character of reds, our choice of color for walls, furniture, accessories, and art is pivotal to the charisma of a home.

When deciding on colors for your home, consider not only your favorite colors but also the color palette as a whole. The colors that represent walls, focal points in a room, and major furniture pieces or window coverings will direct your eye and accentuate those objects that are most important to a room and to you. You don't have to go too far from your own personal delights when choosing colors—go with hues that give you pleasure, not what the design industry has picked for the season. If you have to wait for a wall color to grow on you, it is probably not for you. Think about your favorite colors found in nature and how they work together. They can easily be interpreted for interiors. For example, a scenario of winter trees against a gray-blue sky just before a storm can translate into a pale blue sofa with a deep brown cashmere throw. There are no rules when it comes to choosing colors, so don't be afraid to experiment. However, it is important to know what makes us feel good and what creates a sense of joy and delights the eye.

Although there are no fast rules for choosing colors, different colors do generate certain moods and reactions. For example, cooler blues and greens tend to be tranquil hues, evoking gentle and relaxing feelings and quiet drama. Therefore, sage green, mint green, deep indigo blue, and periwinkle blue are great in bedrooms and other personal spaces.

Also think of the colors in terms of color value. Shades of browns that vary from red-browns to blue-browns will add enough richness and contrast so that all you might need are additional accent colors. An all-white room is very interesting if a variety of whites, from icy-blue white to warm, creamy white, are played off of each other. Often, colors are so subtle that the eye does not pick up the differences. However, when placing different shades of white near each other, their contrasting tones stand out.

Warmer colors, such as yellows, oranges, and reds, are joyful and really about shaking things up. In their primary versions, these are strong and powerful colors, projecting an energetic and exciting ambience, which can be wonderful for living rooms or other rooms for socializing. In their more subtle variations, mustard and ochre yellow or pink and lilac versions of red are more demurely radiant and are perfect in any room.

BELOW

A personal art collection, antiques, and vintage collectables suit this faux-distressed dinning table and create a warm setting for dining and socializing.

OPPOSITE

Natural elements such as plants and flowers, shells, candlelight, and earth materials like raffia, sisal, stone, metal, and wood introduce a calming element to balance the stressful demands of our city lifestyle.

PLEASE TOUCH

The power of touch distinguishes itself from the other senses in that we experience it with our whole being, which can be extremely gratifying. Nerve endings all over our bodies feel tactile pleasures. We respond to touch both physically and emotionally. Receiving a heartfelt hug before leaving for work or walking barefoot on heated stone tile flooring makes us feel good. In our everyday lives at home, there are many pleasures that we experience through the sense of touch. The evolving nature of bathrooms bear witness to this ever-changing concept of comfort and revitalization. Bathrooms were once considered state of the art when toilets, sinks, and bathtubs were standard features. Today, however, the bathtub is not only for washing, but also for rejuvenating, relaxing, and caring for ourselves. Bathrooms have become welcome retreats. Offering more than the option of stretching out, their new designs now feature steps and seats to ensure maximum comfort and are outfitted with pressurized water jets that massage the muscles and reduce stress—water never felt so good. The sensation of being immersed in a Jacuzzi or whirlpool while being massaged by pulsating water or unwinding in a Scandinavian sauna is both revitalizing and refreshing. What could be more soothing after a demanding day at work?

The monochromatic color palettes radiate a sense of tranquility. White is one of the few colors that, when treated holistically and throughout the entire apartment or house, raises little attention. Although not always the most exciting color option, it is the perfect backdrop for all other colors and has a balanced and calming effect.

Fabrics

The appeal of touch is found in the interplay of different textural surfaces. Suede, cashmere, silk, velvet, and raffia all have their own distinct characteristics. Close your eyes and rub your hands across any of these surfaces. Each not only is easily identifiable but also summons up a completely different emotion and association. Whether treating ourselves to the luxury of sleeping on 600-count Egyptian cotton sheets, changing into soft fleece or flannel house clothes at the end of busy workday, or stretching out on a comfy chenille sofa with the remote control, our favorite textures have more influence over our sense of calm than ever before. When incorporating fabrics into a decorating plan, it is wise to take into account not only the colors and patterns of the fabrics but also the character and quality. The fabric is the first level of comfort. A chair covered in velvet or cashmere is spotted as comfortable even before you sit in it. How a fabric feels against your skin is the best test of comfort.

Textures can be key to interpreting different styles, such as African- or Asian-inspired interiors. Rough and tactile elements, such leather, chenille, raffia, wicker, rush, and sea grass, have an earthly connection more credible than cotton, animal-patterned fabrics. Combine these tactile materials with earth tones and you set the stage for a rugged yet refined interpretation of African-inspired interiors. Soft and delicate fabrics such as silk, taffeta, satin, and linen are symbols of luxury and comfort and are perfect to sleep on. Silks, produced by silk worms, are by their very nature luxurious.

Often hand-woven from organic materials, these rather expensive, high-quality fabrics are a sensual delight. In today's market most fabrics are a blend of natural fibers and synthetic materials, such as rayon and polyester, making them more stain resistant and easier to care for but noticeably not as exciting to the touch. However, cotton quilts a little worn with age, cashmere blankets, and other fabrics made from organic fibers are the best to cuddle up with.

SMELL AND TASTE

Aromas, Fragrances, and Smells

The sense of smell is often overlooked as a means of creating mood and a sense of relaxation in our homes. Whether it is a scent from special calming oils used when bathing or from cooking our favorite foods, the effects can work wonders, lifting our spirits and transporting us back to happier times. When you think of exotic fragrances and aromas, places like Bombay, Sicily, and Tunis come to mind—far-away places known not only for their cuisine but

also for the natural ingredients harvested there. The mixture of aromas found in bustling marketplaces filled with herbs, fruits, spices, oils, and flowers is almost mesmerizing. Household smells and scents that are a little closer to home are most often associated with the kitchen. Waking up to the aroma of fresh coffee or coming home to dinner in the oven makes home feel all the more sweeter. The allure of smell and its power to make us feel at home and relaxed are so appreciated today that

Food-related topics—from restaurants, home-cooked meals, and TV cooking shows to chefs and cookbooks—are experiencing an explosion of interest. The power of taste is overwhelming, and it is important that we have the best of foods at home to nourish ourselves both physically and emotionally.

many businesses use it as a marketing approach to relate to customers. The aroma of something delicious greeting you at the door has proven to be an effective way to attract.

The aroma of food is a wonderful conduit for old memories. We all have warm memories and associations with happy times and special occasions that connect with certain foods. The smell of favorite foods is the smell of comfort, a symbol of love and caring. The scent of rosemary, garlic, thyme, and oregano, for example, evokes memories of preparing Thanksgiving feasts and being surrounded by family and friends.

To be met at the door by the fragrance and aroma of scented oils, fresh flowers and herbs, or fresh fruits is a welcoming and rejuvenating experience. We are paying more attention to odors and understanding the positive effect that they have on our emotional and spiritual well-being. Keep bowls of fruits, freshly cut flowers, and flowering plants throughout the house to counteract outside city odors that may find their way indoors.

Creating the Global Urban Mix in Your Home

Today's urban centers are a vibrant mix of people from all corners of the globe. Translating this international blend of cultures into home decor requires that we know something about the regions and lifestyles of the cultures. Therefore, to avoid a museum look, focus on the essence of the culture, its sensitivities, and its attitudes about an array of things from plants and flowers to religion and architecture. This understanding is key to creating contemporary interpretations of these cultures.

Color and Pattern

Applying color and pattern is the easiest and most effective way to create a sensual style. Select hues and tones that best reflect a culture. They can be found in the palettes of textiles, art, and accessories. African textiles incorporate distinctive color combinations and patterns. However, depending on the region of the continent, they can vary from bold primary reds, greens, and blues to soft pastel pinks, aquas, and greens to earthy coffee, copper, beige, and cream. Swedish classical Gustavian design is often characterized by soft blues, white, yellows, and light colored woods, but the later 20th-century Scandinavian design is characterized by fun, bold colors and organic forms of such designers as Josef Frank, Merrimekko, and Stig Lindberg. Think in terms of color palettes—this will give you more opportunity to be creative.

Walls

Carrying the design scheme through to walls with color and pattern will complete the look. Don't be afraid to experiment and test colors. Once the artwork, mirrors, window treatments, and other elements with complementary hues are added, the walls will blend in and recede.

Floors

Floors cover large areas of interiors and help to set the tone. Therefore, take care in choosing their look. Sisal, sea grass, rush, and jute are all popular natural fibers that work well with many decorating styles, as do wood, laminate wood, ceramic tile, and stone. Their neutral colors and textural quality are perfect for any decor.

Art and Design

Select art that makes a credible cultural connection without being a visual cliché. Paintings, figurines, and wall hangings can easily become the focal point of an interior.

Accessories

Accessories are the finishing touches and add character and personality to an interior. A collection of Indonesian jewelry, West African baskets, Japanese sculpture, or English bone china is an easy way to add a personal feel to a room.

Furniture

Imported Chinese armoires, African stools, and Swedish kitchen benches make a cultural statement because of their place of origin, but they also speak to craftsmanship and design as beautiful works of art. The fact that they are functional pieces that you can use every day only increases their value.

Textiles

Upholstery, bed and table linens, window treatments, and wall hangings bring warmth to a space. Tie-dyed Indian silks, Belgian lace, or Cameroonian raffia, whether used on windows or accent furniture, can create a softer look. Fabrics with dominate patterns and motifs are especially beautiful for sofa pillows covers and throws, bed duvets and shams, and tablecloths, napkins, and runners. Many fabrics that are colored with natural dyes may fade under strong light, so avoid long periods of exposure to direct sunlight.

CHAPTER 5

PLACES TO GATHER

The cautionary expression, "You're known for the company you keep," is usually a warning meant to deter us from associating with the wrong kinds of people. Although completely subjective, the adage does underscore the emotional influence and therapeutic effect that others can have upon us, especially that of good friends and family. Adversely, we have all felt the toxic effect of bad relationships and harsh words during disputes. Therefore, as in our social lives, we should take extra care to surround ourselves with those who bring a positive influence into our lives and homes.

Particularly during these unpredictable times that the turn of the century has brought, friendship and companionship have taken on a more meaningful significance. As important as achieving home comforts and tranquility through the use of color, furnishings, and other design elements, surrounding ourselves with the company of friends and family has become an even greater source of spiritual and emotional well-being—and one that is often overlooked. Keeping in contact with our favorite people tips the balance on the comfort scale in our favor and helps fight off stress and the worries of the day.

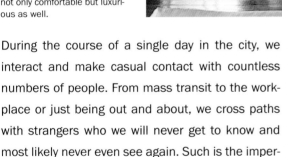

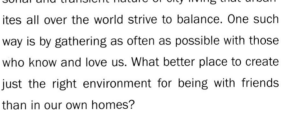

OPPOSITE

Small apartments such as this New York City residence require a flexible furniture plan to accommodate all aspects of life. The smaller the space, the more important the furniture layout. Here, seating is of a smaller scale and easier to move about, but it is, nevertheless, stylishly smart and comfortable, conveying a look and feel that is urban chic.

RIGHT

The beauty and ambience of this living room in Bangkok is perfect for greeting and entertaining guests. Seating is relaxed and comfortable, and there is a large coffee table for dining. Tropical hardwood floors and walls and hand-painted chests and cabinets lovingly displayed create a setting that is not only comfortable but luxurious as well.

During the course of a single day in the city, we interact and make casual contact with countless numbers of people. From mass transit to the workplace or just being out and about, we cross paths with strangers who we will never get to know and most likely never even see again. Such is the impersonal and transient nature of city living that urbanites all over the world strive to balance. One such way is by gathering as often as possible with those who know and love us. What better place to create just the right environment for being with friends than in our own homes?

LIVING ROOMS

The living room remains the room where we usually group the most comfortable sofas and armchairs, our treasured objects of art, and the most functional and attractive lighting. It is, by far, the favorite room in the house for gathering with family and friends. Here we can display our most interesting art, accessories, and collections from travels abroad or from local flea markets. In short, the living room is not only the most beautiful room in the house but also the most flexible for socializing.

Seating Arrangement

When designing for socializing, visualize how friends communicate in your home. What are their favorite chairs, or do they prefer the floor? To which rooms do they gravitate when they just want to casually hang out? Focus on casual placement of seating and furnishings that encourage relaxed conversation. In larger rooms, we often make the mistake of placing furniture pieces far away from each other, trying to spread out them out and cover as much space as possible. Don't be tempted! Intimate and cozy seating arrangements make for easy socializing. Additional space can be used for serving tables or separate seating.

Sofas and chairs should be grouped so that everyone can face each other without obstacles. If there are two sofas, they can face each other. Armchairs should be directly in front of or facing the sofa. Three-seater sofas, though they accommodate the maximum number of guests, are awkward if you are the one sitting in the middle. Unless you're entertaining lots of company and seating is limited, people usually avoid that space.

Mixing Sofas and Chairs

If living room seating consists only of armchairs, they should be arranged in a square or circular pattern with a table, ottoman, or any furniture piece that can substitute for a table in the middle, breaking up the space and providing a surface for displaying objects or serving drinks or food.

Extra seating can have its advantages and disadvantages. Random seating placed around the room can seem somewhat chaotic, especially if you have spent a lot of time and money on decorating and planning a beautiful room. But remember, our friends and family are the whole point of entertaining, so make them as comfortable as possible. Simple and causal entertaining can still be striking and beautiful. As long as the tableware, fresh flowers, linens, and candles are the focus, a dining table with an eclectic mix of several styles of chair can be quite charming. Stackable and folding chairs are a must for larger gatherings and in the garden. They can be casually placed in groups of three to five, just as people naturally congregate.

Tables

Tables should not be too low or too tall. The trend in living room table design is toward a lower height, from 12 to 20 inches (30.5 cm to 51 cm). If you choose one of these contemporary low tables, make sure that the seat of your sofa is proportionately lower as well. Nesting tables, benches, stools, and ottomans, all currently popular, are practical substitutes for the standard coffee table.

It is said that how we entertain can determine how we design, but it can also go the other way, in that our surroundings can influence how we entertain. In this London home, the casual furniture arrangement and eclectic mix of seating styles set the stage for informality and relaxation.

Because coffee tables tend to be multipurpose elements, decisions about them should be made with function in mind. If you sometimes dine in the living room, a taller table, though not quite dining height, can be a good choice. Side and accent tables as well as trolleys and carts provide more flexibility and serving options.

Dining

The combination of good friends, lively conversation, and good food is a joy that should be leisurely savored, in a cheerful and relaxed setting anywhere in the home. There is nothing more enriching to the soul than being surrounded by those we love and enjoying delicious food to nurture the body. The rising popularity of dining, both in restaurants and at home, has inspired city dwellers to experiment with a wide variety of cultural cuisine as well as internationally inspired decoration. From exotic dishes to global design that reflects cultural diversity, the nature of social gathering has become much more fun.

No longer the formal dinners that our parents attended, entertaining today is much more simple and flexible. Guests feel more comfortable preparing and bringing dishes to lessen the work for the host so that everyone has a good time. Casual dinners around a crackling fire or Friday-night pizza and a film allow us to gather for simple, fun relaxation and be ourselves.

Dining Room

In the past, dining rooms were strictly designated as the only place to entertain when serving food. However, as we continually look for ways to simplify our home life and are faced with less time for sit-down dinners with loved ones, dining rooms often go unused. Consequently, these spaces have acquired a stale, often unfriendly character and, consequently, been sacrificed for more functional, everyday activities, such as media rooms, libraries, and family rooms. Although many of us continue to designate the dining room as the

This relaxed yet formal dining room in Singapore, with its serene influence of Chinese purity and simplicity of form, restful spaces around the walls, carpeting under the table for guests, and understated decoration, still reflects a European sense of glamour. The dining and conversations around this table could easily extend into the wee hours of the morning.

main area for gathering and dining, living rooms, kitchens, porches, and the garden are ideal substitutes and are gaining favor.

Table Settings

Whether treating friends to a table of international beers and snacks before an evening out or preparing dinner for ten, simple and unique table arrangements—with an attention to the color palette, style of tableware, texture of table linens, and the fragrance and visual impact of natural elements—can make a visually striking effect and evoke a cheerful and loving atmosphere around a table. Candle votives and a simple Japanese flower arrangement combined on a pared-down Zen-style table setting will do much to relax the pace and soothe the spirit of gathering. With soft-colored saris substituted for a tablecloth and ceramic bowls and trays of exotic fruits, Indian cuisine becomes more than a dining experience when we choose to recreate the look and feel of Bombay. Lowering the height of the table and inviting guests to dine by candlelight while sitting on cozy floor pillows also creates a memorable event.

FOR EVERY ROOM

Focal Points

There is nothing like beautiful and distinctive elements in a room to capture the attention and create interest in a space. Fireplaces are common focal points for a room, as are other architectural features, collections of art, musical instruments, mementos, or even beautiful views of the city. Furniture should be positioned to take advantage of the beautiful features inside and outside the room.

OPPOSITE

No matter how we furnish our homes, we always need more chairs for special occasions. These stackable metal seats look so good that they should always be out and seen, even if they are piled one on top of the other. Stackable chairs never looked so good.

Seating That Is Just Right

Good design doesn't have to be overly comfortable. When entertaining friends, it is not necessary that they sit in the lap of luxury. Firm seats with good back supports are a must. Seating height depends on your comfort level, cultural customs, and design style. In many Asian and Middle Eastern societies, seating is lower to the floor than in Western design. Alternative seating such as futons, ottomans, and stools are typical low seating that have been in the Western scope of design for a long time. However, the current trend in furniture design seems to be moving in a global direction, adopting a more exotic style of wider and lower seats for sofas and armchairs as well. Despite the decorative style, furniture for guests is most effective when kept simple.

Lighting

Lighting is one of the most important elements in creating a friendly and relaxing environment. Its soft and subtle illumination sets the mood, enhances the perception of colors and details, and makes a room feel inviting. Conversely, bland overhead lights can also give the room a completely lifeless and stark appearance, making everything seem flat and unflattering.

Most average-sized rooms require at least four or five lamps—this is especially true for living rooms, which are usually larger than other spaces. Five lamps allow you the functional flexibility for reading, dining, and other activities. There should be a lamp at either end of the sofa, but they need not be two matching table lamps—one could be a floor lamp. A third for other seating and a fourth and fifth source (be them sconces, accent spots, uplights, torches, or cabinet display lighting) for atmosphere. The right combination and variety of lighting is key to how well a space functions and the appropriate mood is created.

ABOVE

Outdoor patios and gardens have the advantage of nature's beauty and spaciousness. Even in a small courtyard garden, there are no windows or doorways to block, so furniture can go anywhere. This Moroccan veranda has been furnished as an indoor interior, with seating for conversation, rugs for comfort, and tapestries and art for beauty and mood.

OPPOSITE

Rooftop decks and gardens, balconies, and fire escapes can be the most dramatic outdoor rooms because of their height. They give us a unique and exciting connection to the city and are great places to gather. The rooftop perspective of this London neighborhood is a view guests might not otherwise see.

RIGHT

At the Morro fort in Havana, a fisherman takes some quiet time for the catch of the day. Once one of the best-protected cities in the New World and the gateway to Latin and South America, Havana was fortified with many forts.

OUTDOORS GATHERING—GREENER OPTIONS

Restricted only by the weather, socializing outdoors—in London's small city backyards, roof decks, and patios, or spacious courtyards and balconies in Bangkok—provides an excellent place to gather and entertain. To be able to look up and see the stars and experience the smell of earth after a summer rain reminds us of our place in the universe.

The charm and spiritual connection of being in natural green spaces is an automatic stress-buster. Add to that a mix of everyday household essentials, such as casual indoor-outdoor furniture, washable floor cushions and mats, and seats made of wicker, rattan, and metal, and the stage is set to a new life beyond our doors.

For apartment dwellers with porches and balconies, flowers, herbs, and vegetable container gardens make the nature connection in more discreet ways. It is amazing how potted plants of various sizes and varieties, a few garden accessories, and a place to sit can transform a small space into a serene garden area.

CHAPTER 6

LIVING AND WORKING AT HOME

Convenience is a distinct benefit of living in the city. What could be better than the luxury of being close enough to your job or the supermarket that you can walk or take city transportation. I can think of only one improvement—working from home. For different reasons, more and more of us are opting to create workspaces at home, a solution that allows more freedom for the way we work and more control over the entire process. You decide the dress code, establish your own pace, and determine what your office will look like. So why are so many opting to leave the corporate structured office? Corporate downsizing is a major factor for a lot of people but so is the lure of striking out on your own and turning what you love to do into a business. For women, who make up the fastest-growing segment of work-at-homers, wanting to be near their young children is a strong incentive. However, the main contributor is the worldwide trend of telecommuting, which over the past several years has gained momentum. In America alone, the number of companies with telecommuting programs is expected to reach 17 million by 2004. This win-win situation offers companies the opportunity to save money on real estate and overhead, and employees get to work in a space that is customized for their personal needs—a perfect solution all around.

LEFT

This small, cozy space, while not the familiar home office, discretely provides a place to make calls, pay bills, and catch up on paperwork.

OPPOSITE

Without sacrificing the flow of this charming and charismatic living room, a desk, desktop computer, task lighting, business phone line, and small storage cabinet were incorporated. Conveniently, the scope of the business was a factor in the conversion.

Who says that a home workspace has to look like an office? The trick in creating a home office is in striking a balance between an efficient and disciplined space that incorporates the latest in technology and, at the same time, a space that is customized to your own sense of aesthetic, lifestyle, and mode of operating. It should be relaxed without being too relaxing. After all, the function here is business. Once you have satisfied the basic essentials, such as office equipment, an appropriately sized work surface, seating, task lighting, and storage, you just have to decide on a decorative style.

OPPOSITE

Rooms that serve a dual function, such as this bedroom-home office, sometimes require some sort of partition to separate them. Often it is not any specific distraction but rather the idea of sharing a space that warrants a partition. Portable room dividers in the form of standing screens, armoires, or fabric panels are also appropriate and effective partitions.

ABOVE

Fully equipped, efficiently run home offices can go anywhere and do not take up a lot of space. As long as they have all of the office components, the look, size, and location can vary drastically, as this balcony office overlooking the main entrance illustrates.

CARVING OUT A SPACE

For young singles with small apartments or anyone living alone, allotting space is not so difficult because there is no one else to consider—your office can go almost anywhere. A living room, dining room, or spare bedroom can provide an easy solution. You may, however, want to avoid placing an office in your own sleeping quarters. It could prove to be too restful an environment for an effective workstation.

Also, you may want to keep this room dedicated to relaxing and prevent the toxic stress of everyday work concerns from invading your place of slumber. In addition, after showering and getting ready for the day, it is nice to have somewhere to go, even if it is only down the hall.

A DIFFERENT KIND OF CORNER OFFICE

The main obstacle for creating a home office in the heart of the city is having enough space. The size and scope of a home office depend on how much space is available for conversion and the nature of the business or scope of services you offer. The ideal scenario is to create an independent, separate room that is large enough to accommodate a work area with storage files and equipment.

However, because we cannot always sacrifice an entire bedroom or living room, one solution is reconfiguring and dividing these same rooms and creating a new multipurpose area with the office in the corner. With the efficient use of wall space for shelving, storage, foldable furnishings, and good lighting, corner spaces can be very effective.

Tucked away far enough to allow for privacy and quiet, this lofty home office is still very much a part of the home, complete with a view of the lower level.

PRIVACY AND QUIET

Another obstacle to working at home is creating the privacy and quiet that is needed for concentration. It is important during the course of the day to talk on the phone and possibly meet with others undisturbed. Therefore, in a room with a dual function, portable partitions, flexible furniture arrangements, moveable storage units, or even tall plants may be enough to create visual separation of space, as needed. Standing screen partitions are a simple and effective way to visually block out the remainder of the room. In the city, where loud and persistent noise is an ongoing concern, it is not always easy to block outdoor traffic and other sounds of the city, or even to dampen indoor noise from the rest of the household. If your workspace is in a separate room, simply closing the door is the easiest solution. However, in a shared space, the best approach is making the office itself as quiet as possible through the use of textiles and padding. Fabric goes a long way in absorbing sound. Padded partitions covered with fabric, rugs, or carpets do much to quiet a space. Soundproofing your windows is another effective way of blocking out unwanted street noise. Today's technology allows us to block out up to 90 percent of outside noises. Installed by professionals, soundproof windows are made up of laminated glass with an inner layer of plastic that resists window vibration. This installation is a worthwhile investment for a home office that requires focus and quiet.

This city loft apartment can easily accommodate a spacious home office. The functional floor-to-ceiling cabinet storage is so beautifully made that it is also the room's design focus. The large area rug defines the office area and anchors the furnishing, which would have disappeared into the same-color floor. Well organized and down to the basics, this home office has a look of efficiency.

Is It a Home or an Office?

Does a home office have to look like an office to be businesslike? Don't be in such a rush to create the standard office at home. A common observation of corporate offices around the world is that they are boring and dull. Consisting of stacked floors in high-rises, outfitted with standard floor plans for lots of employees, offices are usually soulless places that have very little personal character. It is hard to envision such a space in our homes. Conversely, the most convincing argument for setting up a home office is that we get to make it exactly as we want. It can be beautiful, more relaxing, and more like our home. With that in mind, take advantage of all that our personal lifestyle and casual home environments have to offer. Low-tech 1920s vintage furniture and high-tech fiber optics communication are a very creative combination.

Whatever the design style of your home, carry it through to your office in a seamless flow. A blend of home style and corporate influence is what working at home is all about. Accessories such as photos, mementos, and objects that express who you are lend a sense of intimacy and emotional comfort. A mohair throw and extra-comfy seating are a welcome retreat for an afternoon break. Neutral color schemes, fabrics, and carpets that are used throughout the home can work just as well in the office. A turn-of-the-century vintage secretary or a 1950s Finn Juhl table used as a work surface may be appropriate, depending on the nature of the work. A comfortable chair with good back support, one that is sufficient for sitting and working from 9:00 to 5:00 is a must. If there is one vestige of the corporate world to survive the move to the home office, it is office seating. Somewhat pricey but well worth it, the new generation of office seating is losing the dull, corporate look and comes with innovative ergonomic features that make sitting at a desk quite pleasurable. Whatever your choice of chair, whether it is a well-proportioned armchair or a simple dining chair, make sure that at the end of the day you can still sit comfortably.

OPPOSITE

Beauty and function come together in the design of this home office desk and credenza. The free-form, frosted-glass top and the asymmetrical design give this desk a whimsical spirit and make even the most challenging of paperwork a little lighter.

ABOVE

Colorful and modern-styled desks and storage units arranged in an all-white room can help define your office space and make it more fun to work in. Keeping everything organized is important when meeting with clients.

ORGANIZATION

An effective means of carrying the sense of calm and easy living created throughout your home into the workplace is through organization. You can achieve this by simplifying and editing out all the things not necessary for conducting daily business and getting the job done. Being so close to all those personal things that give us pleasure can make it difficult to refrain from accumulating everything from magazines and CDs to snacks and a miniature refrigerator. Visually conveying credibility and control, organization is crucial to a successful business. A cluttered desk is the last thing a client wants to see. Simple, sturdy, and spacious cabinets discreetly keep everything under wraps and give the space an even smarter and efficient appearance.

Storage and surfaces for fax machines, phones, copiers, computers, and printers should be key considerations in the planning of the office. Cabinets, armoires, and room dividers with storage are stylish variations that work as well as standard cabinets. However, for maximum storage in a minimal space, wall-mounted, floor-to-ceiling cabinet units are the most efficient choice.

Easy-to-clean surfaces, a minimum of clutter, and low-maintenance furniture are some of the
elements of a healthy urban
home.

Creating the Healthy City Home

Simplify and Edit

In every area of the home, simplify and give yourself room to be. When decorating, make room for the things that really matter and eliminate space fillers. A certain amount of clutter can be charming, but it has its price. Keeping up with the dust and dirt that settles is time-consuming and often gets overlooked.

Ventilation

Air quality is more of an issue during the winter months. Even then, it is important to open the windows periodically to infuse your home with fresh air.

Natural Air Cleaners

Houseplants can play a role in controlling contaminants and pollutants in our homes that cause headaches and sinus congestion. Research shows that houseplants (such as the peace lily, Boston fern, bamboo palm, rubber plant, and gerbera daisy) counteract substances that cause poor indoor air quality. Several 10-inch (25.5 cm) pots per room will improve your air quality.

Humidifiers and Air Purifiers

Higher temperatures generated by heaters in tightly sealed winter homes make the air ripe for bacteria, pet dander, and dust, causing dry skin, parched throats, and itchy eyes. Humidifiers and air purifiers are important for keeping air moist and clean, especially during the winter months. A humidifier/vaporizer (the cold-mist type) can breed biological allergens, so make sure to change the water every day.

Removing Shoes at the Front Door

Asians, Scandinavians, and Muslims, no matter where they may live around the world, continue to practice the custom of taking off their shoes at the front door. This centuries-old tradition serves two purposes. First, it keeps the dirt and germs that we collect on our shoes during the course of the day from getting tracked through the rest of the home—something that most of us in the West do not consider. Secondly, it has the metaphorical significance of emotionally separating the outside world from the private, separate world of home.

Area Rugs and Carpets

Removable floor coverings, which can be cleaned and returned, are excellent for maintaining good air quality at home, especially in bedrooms and other rooms where children spend lots of time. Easy-care floor coverings will have noticeable positive results.

Washable Floors

Wood, laminate, tile, marble, and vinyl floors, which can be regularly washed down, not only keep a room fresh and clean but also give it a spacious feeling.

Pet Places

As soon as we close the door behind us, the first thing our pets do is curl up on the most comfortable chair or sofa. There is not too much we can do about it, so if you are not willing to place chairs on your sofa or remove the seat cushions every time you leave, invest in some throws with which to cover the furniture. They can be regularly washed and replaced. This will save your furniture and keep pet dander to a minimum.

Cozy corners are what many of us identify with when we think of curling up with a good book or settling down for a quiet moment. A comfortable chair, good light source (the more natural light, the better), a side table to hold a drink or the latest magazine, and some kind of screen or door to close out everyday activity can create the perfect environment for relaxation.

CHAPTER 7

PLACES JUST TO BE

The Power of Home

We are increasingly learning more about the causes and effects of stress and how it influences us, not only mentally and emotionally but physically as well. Particularly, the frenetic pace of everyday urban life leaves city folk even more vulnerable to stress from every direction. However, the good news is that we are also learning more about the ways and means to lessen and eliminate its occurrence and effects through a holistic and peaceful home environment and relaxing lifestyle.

Over the past decade, meditation, yoga, and other mind-body exercises have experienced a tremendous growth in interest as techniques for recovering physical, mental, and spiritual health. Today, Western physicians acknowledge that meditation leads to the reduction of chronic pain, anxiety, cholesterol levels, and blood cortisol levels, as well as improved sleeping patterns and, most important, the reduction of high blood pressure. The practice of meditation and the healthy lifestyle that accompanies it make a holistic connection to the look and feel of our personal spaces. Harmonious and personal spaces where we can relax, recollect our thoughts, pray, and commune with our inner selves have to be designated both inside and outside of our homes, furnished and decorated to accommodate such a lifestyle.

In the heart of Boston, this intimate urban garden has found the key to tranquility in the middle of the city. The gravel and stone walkway provides a gentle entrance to a relaxing place to escape with a good book, to do some gardening, or to take time for prayer or meditation. This garden retreat affirms the holistic nature of urban home life, even in our densely populated cities.

COMFORT ZONES

Quiet Home Zones

Over the past decade, Western designers have taken notice and responded to what has been known for centuries among the Asian cultures: How we furnish and accessorize our personal living spaces has a major influence on our emotional and spiritual health. The approach that we take in decorating our homes can help find the balance between our worries and concerns. In every home there should be a space where we can take time for ourselves and just be. It doesn't have to be a separate room—maybe it is a quiet corner for reading or a bathroom adorned with fragrant candles, special oils, and plants. Gardens, porches, balconies, decks, or quiet corners in a bedroom or library—all have the potential to be a revitalizing comfort zone. The common denominator for all these spaces is that they encourage us to do whatever we need to relax and unwind. For example, if you like to read, choose a private space, no matter how small, to curl up with lots of good books and magazines. A comfy chair or some down-filled floor pillows will do.

No matter how much we love being in the company of family and friends, there comes a time when the privacy of our own company is just what we need, quality time that allows us to reverse the chaos of the day through the practice of yoga, escaping into a generous window seat with a good book, or an afternoon of baking in a cozy kitchen. Such are the kinds of areas that should be considered when designing and decorating city home interiors. The whole notion of relaxation and quiet time is gaining credibility as barometers for good quality of life, so much so that many doctors agree that meditating, doing hobbies, listening to music, or gathering with friends and family are valid methods of destressing. Fortunately, the decorating styles that accommodate quiet zones are as varied as the urban population. Think about the colors that emotionally transport us, textures that caress, and forms that are simple and uncomplicated.

City Gardens

Today, backyards, roof decks, balconies, porches, patios, and gardens are contributing a new dimension to urban living in the form of therapeutic spaces and uniting our more spiritual side to the green environment. This holistic view of city living spaces has transformed the urban garden into an integral part of daily space. With the exception of seasonal climate and fluctuation of everyday weather, there are few limitations to how our courtyards, rooftop gardens, backyards, and other outdoor areas can be used. Perhaps it is the pleasure of finally harvesting fresh herbs and vegetables for dinner, dozing off to a bird's serenade, or practicing yoga in the early morning that these green zones are proving to be a welcome relief.

For city dwellers in particular, this trend toward outdoor living is a welcome opportunity not only to expand our living space but, more importantly, to connect and take advantage of all the healing elements that Mother Nature has to offer. As we look to our homes for greater comfort and calm, this renewed perspective on outdoor-indoor spaces offers simple yet rewarding pleasures that are crucial to the harmonious balance of our urban lifestyle.

Not too long ago, gardens and other green spaces that surrounded our homes were valued only for their aesthetic extra square footage and curbside appeal. Ornamental gardens were designed to be seen and admired, to beautify a home, and to

enhance its resale value. Except for the occasional barbecue and family gatherings, backyards and gardens were seldom appreciated as more than an amenity. Following in the footsteps of ancient Chinese private gardens designed as spiritual utopias, places where one could commune with nature and the inner self, to medieval European alchemy gardens, which were created for the sole purpose of medical healing, we in the West are experiencing a growing enthusiasm for the recreational, spiritual, and culinary joys of gardening.

Whether a New York rooftop garden or a courtyard in Fez, the love of gardening has as much to do with nurturing our souls and spirit as it does cultivating flowers beds. From experienced full-time gardeners tending traditional flower gardens to those of us with less time who prefer low-maintenance gardens with a wider variety of plants, these green zones reflect our personality.

OPPOSITE

Tranquil spaces are where we make them. Of course, a separate room would be ideal. However, if you choose the right time of the day when life is quiet, this can be the time for repose and relaxation. This tranquil apartment living room, with its oversized sofa on which to stretch out and listen to music or the floor-to-ceiling windows to greet the day with a salute to the sun, has the elements of a home comfort zone.

LEFT

Even a spacious living room can have its moments of quiet and calm. When the fire is roaring and an easy chair and ottoman beckon us to relax, take a deep breath, and exhale.

Not only a means of hygiene, bathing in Japan is often considered a spiritual experience, where one can reflect on the day. Beautiful wooden tubs such as this are much deeper than Western tubs and are filled with very hot water. Washing away the stresses of the day and improving circulation are the wellness benefits of the bath.

The Home Spa

The power of the bathtub for reclining, the elements of water and steam, the addition of aromatic oils, the intimacy of candlelight and privacy—all make today's bathroom a true sanctuary as well as the most relaxing retreat in the home. Although we all have them, often we do not have or make the time to take advantage of them. A quick shower and a couple of minutes to blow-dry hair and apply makeup every morning can make it feel like the most hectic space in the home. At the end of a stressful day is when we usually need a calming and leisurely bath. To fully enjoy bathing and take advantage of the healing and therapeutic energy of water, steam, and aromas, we must rethink our idea of the bathroom and how it can provide emotional, physical, and spiritual balance in our everyday urban lives.

Set aside and plan your evening as you would for a regular trip to the gym or watching your favorite TV show. There are several traditional bath customs from around the world that have proven to be restorative and effective. The Japanese bath, the Turkish steam bath, the Native American sweat lodge, and the Finnish sauna are the most well-known. Some of them we can re-create in our own homes; for others, it is impossible. However, identifying with and understanding the ancient art of bathing can be inspirational for creating those spaces just to be. Choose essential oils such as chamomile, frankincense, and lavender to sooth and unwind, or mint and lemon for memory enhancement and mental focus. Select scented candles and bath salts and enjoy the calming environment that the soft light creates. Plants are also welcome natural elements and add to the organic and spiritual nature of the bathroom spa.

Japanese Baths: Water Not Just for Washing In Japan, bathing continues to offer spiritual contentment through the cleansing of the spiritual body and sumptuous enjoyment. Aesthetically, Japanese bathtubs made of wood are exquisite. Generally much deeper than their Western counterparts, they

The spiritual character and attention to comfort as benefits of high technology is revealed in this futuristic bathroom. Clean lines, minimal forms, and uncomplicated color palettes all lend a soothing and peaceful character to this space. Calla lilies make the perfect accessory.

BELOW

The polished finishes and minimal design of this bathroom's fixtures create the look and feel of sensual luxury down to the details.

are filled with near-steaming water. For at least half an hour each day, the evenings are spent submerged to the neck in very hot water. Traditionally, bathing in Japan is not necessarily about washing, as this is done before getting into the tub, but rather bathing is a means of relaxing at the end of the day and stimulating circulation, which the hot water can facilitate.

Japanese Hot Springs The more than 2,000 hot springs in Japan continue to be popular with its cit-

izens. Renowned for medicinal purposes, ancient hot springs contain sulfur, calcium, sodium, and other minerals that fight high blood pressure, diabetes, and arthritis. These benefits, in addition to the soothing nature of the bubbling hot water, make this ancient bathing tradition as popular as ever among the Japanese, young and old.

Turkish Hot Air Baths Another traditional type of bath is the Turkish bath. Its history extends to the time of the Romans. Similar to the sauna, Turkish

The privacy of the bathroom makes it the perfect home sanctuary, even when you're not bathing. A sumptuous chaise and armchair add all the comfort you need to nourish the spirit and take time for yourselves.

baths are also steam baths, with the same principle—that steam and sweat eliminate toxins from the skin and help us to relax. However, they also include massage to cleanse and remove dead skin and to improve circulation. Designed for the general public, these bathhouses were beautiful structures, often in the form of rotundas. Although it may not be possible to duplicate the Turkish bath technique in our home, it casts a new light on the role of hot air and cleansing.

Scandinavian Saunas If you are lucky enough to have a sauna in your home, you undoubtedly appreciate the relaxing and rejuvenating power of steam. Today's portable models are easily installed indoors or, as they were traditionally located, outdoors. This centuries-old Finnish and Swedish bathing custom consists of a wooden shed outfitted with multitiered benches for sitting and reclining. Steam, the main

A warm bath or hot shower at the end of the day can often put everyday stresses in proper perspective, making the bathroom the most peaceful room in our home. More than for washing, this sensual and serene indoor/outdoor bath in Singapore features a generous marble bathtub and shower and enough tranquil space to meditate or spend some peaceful time.

source of heat and humidity, is produced by sprinkling water on hot rocks, filling the small space with hot air, close to 200 degrees Fahrenheit (93 degrees centigrade). Designed primarily for cold climate locales, the cozy atmosphere of a toasty sauna is a welcome relief on a chilly winter day.

This custom of steam bathing not only opens the pores so that your skin gets a thorough cleansing, but it also has other valuable and far-reaching effects on the body, such as improving circulation, relieving arthritic pain, burning calories, and, above all, relaxing muscles and reducing stress. Just make sure you drink plenty of water to replace that lost through perspiration.

All of the baths share a similarity—millions of people around the world reap physical benefits and improve their emotional, spiritual, and physical state of health.

Whether we bathe Japanese style, have a Finnish sauna installed in our apartment, or hire a masseur for a deep massage, we must take the time to indulge ourselves and partake in a holistic approach to a balanced lifestyle.

Tranquil places in the home can begin at the entrance. The soft glow of filtered light, walls covered with natural fiber, reflective stone floor, intricate stone masonry, and a monochromatic color scheme express a home with attention to the emotional, as well as physical, comforts of home.

Quiet Corners

If lack of space in your home rules out the possibility of creating a separate room as a private retreat, quiet corners and other small spaces that offer a degree of privacy from other activity in the room can easily be carved out of existing interiors. These unexpected nooks and corners are defined mostly by the choice and placement of furniture, standing screens, or plants for privacy. When choosing the furniture for this space, think about what is comfortable; style is secondary. Chairs or chaises in which you could recline and dose off for hours are perfect, as are ottomans or poufs on which to rest your feet. A side table to rest a drink, food, or earphones is also necessary. Also, the element of sunlight is critical to the tranquil nature of a quiet corner. The light should be bright enough and direct enough to read by. And if you like to read, keep lots of books and magazines nearby.

Relaxing Spaces

Reading Spaces

Whether it is perusing the evening newspaper, catching up with monthly magazines, or escaping into the world of a lengthy novel, reading is one of the most popular leisure pastimes enjoyed by young and old. To sit back and lose ourselves in a good novel, pick up the daily newspaper and see what is happening in the world, or investigate new recipes in a cookbook is sometimes all we need to rejuvenate and recover from the stresses of the day. The right conditions, such as a space that is out of the way with as few distractions as possible, allow us to devote our full attention to reading and the chance to truly relax. Other changes that make our personal reading retreats even more enjoyable and relaxing are a comfy chair with pillows, a side table, a window that allows natural light, a small bookcase filled with our most recent favorite books and magazines, and soft music or just the quiet.

Quiet Corners

If space allows, a small room for daytime reading is the beginning of the perfect reading retreat. However, a corner in a room that we seldom use or bedroom will do for most. Some prefer to close out the day with something to read in bed. As long as the space is calm, it will make a good reading space.

The Perfect Chair

For those who can spend hours with a good book, a comfy chair is crucial. Such seats should allow you to relax as you like. The choice of seating could be a chaise, recliner, club chair with ottoman, or futon. The challenge is in not choosing a chair that is so comfortable that we doze off immediately.

Small Side Tables

Very seldom do we only read when we settle down with an evening paper or a good magazine. An accompanying table with easy access to hold a cup of tea, a snack, or other reading material makes the reading space much more accommodating and keeps the time and attention devoted to the relaxation of reading and not inconveniently searching and reaching for things.

Lighting

Make sure that you have good task lighting that is functional for reading. A serviceable lamp will prove to be more valuable than a great-looking design that provides general lighting. Ample natural light is perfect for daytime reading.

Sofa

If you like to stretch out on your sofa to read, make sure you have good support. Soft, down-filled throw pillows make a relaxing nest, but if the goal is to stay awake, find that balance of comfort. Sofas with lower, padded arms are best with a pillow.

Outdoor

Gardens, porches, and balconies can be the best reading retreats. In the city, however, it is not as easy to control the noise level. Whereas the automobile traffic and sirens might dominate, some sounds can be quite calming—the rustle of trees and singing birds, for example. If you choose the right time of day in your neighborhood, such as Saturday or Sunday mornings, even in the busiest of cities, the outdoors can be the perfect place to enjoy a cup of coffee and the morning paper.

10 Corso Como
Corso Como 10
Milano 20154
Italy 654831
39 02 290 13581
02 29 00 26 74 (fax)

Designer home accessories, clothing, and art

ABC Carpet and Home
888 Broadway
New York, NY 10003
United States
212 473 3000
www.abccarpetandhome.com

Everything for the home from around the world

Afro Art
Hornsgatan 58
118 21 Stockholm
Sweden
46 (0) 8 642 5095

Textiles, ceramics, and crafts from Africa, Latin America, and Asia

America Antiques and Design
5 S. Main St.
Lambertville, NJ 08530
United States

609 397 6966
www.americadesigns.com
Designer: David Teague

20th-century and custom furniture and accessories

Anthropologie
201 W. Lancaster Ave.
Wayne, PA 19087
United States
610 687 4141

Home furnishings, clothing, personal accessories, and gifts

Baker Knapp and Tubbs
One Design Center Place, Suite 300
Boston, MA 02210
United States

Contemporary and classic furniture, lighting, and accessories

Black Ink Home
370 Broadway
Cambridge, MA 02139
United States
617 576 0707

Industrial-style lamps, furniture, and rugs

Bo Concept
571 Mount Pleasant Ave.
Livingston, NJ 07039
United States
Sj@club8usa
www.boconcept.com

Contemporary Danish home furnishings

The Conran Shop
55 Marylebone High St.
London, W1U 5HS
United Kingdom
020 7723 2223
www.conran.co.uk

Clark's Case
Hornsgatan 68
SE 118 21 Stockholm
Sweden
46 (0)8 668 00 29
www.clarkscase.com

Urban contemporary furniture and accessories, interior design

Crate & Barrel
1 800 996 9960
www.crateandbarrel.com

Urban contemporary furniture and home goods

Dane Decor Downtown
315 Arch St.
Philadelphia, PA 19100
United States
215 922 2104

Contemporary European furnishings and home accessories

Designers Guild
267-271 Kings Rd.
London SW3 5EN
United Kingdom
(020) 7351 5775
Designer: Tricia Guild

Linens, soft finishes, wallpaper, furniture

Divertimenti
45-47 Wigmore St.
London W1H 9LE
United Kingdom
(020) 7935 0689

Lifestyle, Italian, French, and English kitchenwares

Djema Imports
70 W. 125 St.
New York, NY 10027
United States
212 289 3842

African woven textiles and print fabrics

Donghia Furniture/Textiles, ltd
485 Broadway
New York, NY 10013- 5901
United States
1 800 DONGHIA

www.donghia.com

Ethniciti
668 N. High St.
Columbus, OH 43215
United States
614 222 6700

Home accessories and art from Africa, South America, and North America

Fosters
124 N. 3rd St.
Philadelphia, PA 19100
United States
267 671 0588

Gourmet cookware and urban homeware

Habitat
196 Tottenham Court
London W1P 9LD
United Kingdom
(020) 7631 3880
www.habitat.net

Furniture, homewares, and bed linens

Heals
196 Tottenham Court
London W1P 9LD
United Kingdom
(020) 7636 1666

Furniture, lighting, and tabletop accessories

Henry Calvin (to the trade only)
2046 Lars Way
Medford, OR 97501
United States
888 732 1996

Fine upholstery and window textiles

Herman Miller
One Design Center Place, Suite 734
Boston, MA 02210
United States
617 956 4100

Classic modern design and contemporary office furniture

House Drottinggatan
Drottinggatan 81
11160 Stockholm
Sweden
08 406 06 81

Home furnishings, textiles, lighting, and other accessories

IKEA
1 800 434 IKEA
www.IKEA.com

Contemporary furniture and home accessories

Indigo Arts
151 N. 3rd St.
Philadelphia, PA 19106
United States
215 922 4041, 1 888 indiart
www.indigoarts.com

Home accessories, art and crafts from around the world

International Visions Gallery
2629 Connecticut Ave.
Washington, D.C. 20008
United States
202 234 5112
www.inter-visions.com

Original paintings, sculpture, and photography

Jacksons 20th Century Design
Tyska brinken 20
111 27 Stockholm
Sweden
46 08 411 8587

20th-century furniture, accessories, and art

Klara
Nytorgsgatan 36
11640 Stockholm
Sweden
46 (0) 8 694 9240
46 (0) 8 611 5252 (fax)

Contemporary Scandinavian furniture, textiles, porcelain design

Kubatana Gallery
1831 Peachtree Rd.,NE
Atlanta, GA 30309
United States
404 355 5764
www.kubatana.com

African and African-American paintings, sculpture, ceramics, and more

Laura Ashley Ltd.
27 Bagleys Lane
Fulham, London
SW6 2QA
United Kingdom
020 7880 5100
www.lauraashley.com

Material Culture
4700 Wissahicken Ave.
Philadelphia, PA 19144
United States
215 849 8030
www.materialculture.com

Furnishings and folk art from around the world

The Menagerie LTD (to the trade)
2400 Market St., Suite 323
Philadelphia, PA 19103
United States
215 561 5041

Period and contemporary home furnishings

Mosaic
122 Hudson St.
New York, NY 10013
United States
646 613 8570

African-style furnishings, tribal art, and colorful textile

Nomad
1741 Massachusetts Ave.
Cambridge, MA 02140-2217
United States
617 497 6677

Global home accessories, clothing, and personal accessories

Osbourne & Little (to the trade only)
90 Commerce Rd.
Stamford, CT 06902
United States
203 359 1500

Fine textiles

Padouk Designs
www.padoukdesign.com
Designers Epee Ellong and Diane Chehab

*Design and African-inspired
furnishings*

Posh on Tremont
524 Tremont St.
Boston, MA 02118
United States
617 338 7222

*Contemporary urban and vintage home
accessories*

Pucci
44 West 18th St.
New York, NY 10011
United States
212 633 0452

*Italian classic and modern furnishings
and accessories*

Repertoire
75 Grand St.
New York, NY 10013
United States
212 219 8159
www.repertoire.com

International designer furniture

RMMR
433 West 14th St.
New York, NY 10014
United States
212 414 0488

*French inspired furniture and
accessories*

Roche Bobois
15-18 rue de Lyon
Paris75012
France
01 53 46 10 20
www.roche-bobois.com

*Barcelona, Boston, Miami, Paris,
Washington D.C.*

R.O.O.M.
Almstromergatan 20
10028 Stockholm
Sweden
46 (0)8 692 50 00
www.room.se

*Contemporary home furnishings, textiles,
accessories, and gifts*

Scan Furniture
1 800 386 0989
www.scanfurniture.com

*Classic, modern, and contemporary home
furnishings and accessories*

Svensk Tenn
Strandvagen 5
Stockholm
Sweden
46 (0) 8670 1600

*Traditional and contemporary Swedish
furniture, porcelain, textiles, and
accessories*

Taji Modern
62 N. 3rd St.
Philadelphia, PA 19106
United States
215 922 2757

Antiques and collectibles

Tufenkian Tibetan Carpets
902 Broadway, 2nd Floor
New York, NY 10010-6002
United States
212 475 2475

*Contemporary and traditional hand-
woven, global-inspired carpet collection*

Twist
1134 Pine St.
Philadelphia, PA 19107
United States
215 925 1242
www.insidedesignltd.com
Interior designers: Lisa Formica and
Sharne Algotsson

*Vintage and contemporary furnishings,
home accessories, and personal care
products*

Urban Archeology
One Design Center Place, Suite 342
Boston, MA 02210
United States
617 737 4646

Designer and custom lighting

Usona Home Furnishings
223 Market St.
Philadelphia, PA 19106
United States
215 351 9160
www.usonahome.com

*Contemporary furniture, lighting, art, and
accessories*

Uzoamaka
1532 Sansom St., 2nd Floor
Philadelphia, PA 19103
United States
215 832 0060

*Accessories, textiles, arts, and gifts from
Africa and around the world*

YU
15 Greene Ave.
Brooklyn, NY 11238
United States
718 237 5878

*Asian antiques, contemporary furnish-
ings, and home accessories*

Zimmer + Rohde (to the trade only)
Zimmermuhlenweg 14-16
61440 Oberursel/Frankfurt
Germany
6171 632 02
www.zimmer-rohde.com

Zoe
279 Newbury St.
Boston, MA 02116
United States
617 375 9135

*Contemporary furniture and home
accessories*

PHOTOGRAPHER CREDITS

Björg, 6; 18; 19 (bottom); 111

ColePrévost, Inc., 130; 131

Guillaume DeLaubier, 22; 24; 40; 56; 62;
63; 64; 68; 75; 79; 80; 85; 87; 93;
96; 97; 101; 102; 104; 106; 121;
132; 135

Carlos Domenech/www.domenechphoto
.com/Celia Domenech, 83

Carlos Domenech/www.domenechphoto
.com/Fanny Haim, Design, 23; 136

Carlos Domenech/www.domenechphoto
.com/L Studio, Miami, 43; 59; 67; 107

Michael Freeman, 11; 41; 51; 78; 98;
112; 128

Hameed Gorani/ColePrévost, Inc., 109

Benjamin Harris, B.S.K., 19 (top)

Nestor Hernandez, 2; 13; 103

Kubatana Gallery/Courtesy of *Homes of
Color* magazine, 69

Kjell Johansson, 15

John Edward Linden/Mark Guard, 55

Ray Main/www.mainstreamimages.co.uk,
8; 110; 115

Courtesy of Roche Bobois, 49; 52; 61;
71; 88; 116; 119; 126; 138

George Ross, 144

Eric Roth, 16 (right); 21; 81; 122; 124

Eric Roth/Charles Spada, Design, 39

Courtesy of Scan Furniture, 117

Gunnar Smoliansky, 17

Simon Upton/The Interior Archive, 47;
48;

Peter Vanderwarker/Courtesy of Flavin
Architects, 26-35

Paul Warchol, 36; 38; 91; 92; 95

Doug Weissman, 16 (left); 20

Luke White/The Interior Archive, 10; 25;
61; 72; 127

Andrew Wood/The Interior Archive, 44;
76; 77; 100; 108

ABOUT THE AUTHOR

Interior designer, stylist, and author Sharne Algotsson specializes in global and urban spaces. She has recently co-launched Twist, a lifestyle store and interior design consultancy in center city Philadelphia, which specializes in comforts of all kinds for the home. She is coauthor of *The Spirit of African Design* and author of *African Style, Down to the Details* (Clarkson Potter).